"Randy Lundy's poems summon pathways between the past, present, and future, thus realigning our connection to land, memory, and history. This book is a ceremony we will 'drag our heaviness into,' a 'lodge [that] reveals the dark knowing of the body.' Field Notes offers readers an often startling but necessary glimpse of our changing world."—SHERWIN BITSUI, author of *Dissolve*

"'You will think of mistahi-maskwa locked up in Stony Plain bearing the pain of his people, and of Bodhidharma crossing the mountains bearing the teachings.' This is the book of a man threading his way between plenitude and emptiness, between private histories and public memory, at once in solitary meditation and in the company of his dogs, the dead, the varied birds, and always the land, in all its moods and seasons."
—ROO BORSON, author of *Cardinal in the Eastern White Cedar*

"There is a scalpel-like precision at the heart of Randy Lundy's latest collection, *Field Notes for the Self*. The poet dissects the quotidian moments that make up a life and in so doing reveals how darkness and light are in constant relationship. As readers, we are nudged to consider not only how each poem is a brief, dazzling illumination but how the dark they disappear into is just as powerful and relevant as the light they momentarily reveal."—EVE JOSEPH, author of *Quarrels*

"Lundy is a survivor and much of that survival stems from his ability to see nature as the most important healer in his life. We, the readers, are lucky to see how the best and worst experiences in his life are transformed into poetry. His poems light our way forward as only the highest form of art can do."
—DUANE NIATUM, author of *Earth Vowels*

ᐃᓇᑲ

OSKANA POETRY & POETICS

Randy Lundy

*Field Notes
for the Self*

University of Regina Press

Cover art: Drawing by Duncan Noel Campbelll, based on the Montana Hellgate Canyon pictographs.

Cover and text design: Duncan Campbell, University of Regina Press

Editor: Jan Zwicky
Proofreader: Donna Grant

The text and titling faces are Arno, designed by Robert Slimbach.

creative
SASKATCHEWAN

Library and Archives Canada Cataloguing in Publication

Title: Field notes for the self / Randy Lundy.

Names: Lundy, Randy, 1967- author.

Series: Oskana poetry & poetics.

Description: Series statement: Oskana poetry & poetics

Identifiers: Canadiana (print) 20190187832 | Canadiana (ebook) 20190187867 | ISBN 9780889776913 (softcover) | ISBN 9780889776951 (PDF)

Classification: LCC PS8573.U54398 F54 2020 | DDC C811/.54—dc23

10   9   8   7   6   5   4   3   2   1

UNIVERSITY OF REGINA PRESS
University of Regina
Regina, Saskatchewan
Canada S4S 0A2
TELEPHONE: (306) 585-4758
FAX: (306) 585-4699
WEB: www.uofrpress.ca
EMAIL: uofrpress@uregina.ca

We acknowledge the support of the Canada Council for the Arts for our publishing program. We acknowledge the financial support of the Government of Canada. / Nous reconnaissons l'appui financier du gouvernement du Canada. This publication was made possible with support from Creative Saskatchewan's Book Publishing Production Grant Program.

for Caroline Bighetty & Marie & William Douglas,
even though I never knew you, kâhkiyaw niwahkômâkanak

The human being has two states of consciousness: one in this world, the other in the next. But there is a third state between them, not unlike the world of dreams, in which we are aware of both worlds, with their sorrows and joys.

—BRIHADARANYAKA UPANISHAD

Thus do we slide into our disbelief
                              and disaffection,
Caught in the weeds and understory of our own lives,
Bad weather, bad dreams.
Proper attention is our refuge now, our perch and our praise.

—CHARLES WRIGHT

CONTENTS

The leaves on the elm across the street, quivering
like trout pulled from a stream. Light streams
like water streams from fins, and *gleam*, that's
the word you're looking for.

The word refers to that shine on the face
just when spirit departs. Yes, when it leaves.
That is the word you are looking for.

You should not have looked on your tongue.
Wrong place, my friend. Think about
that 3000-year-old bowl with cheese
baked into its depression,

while the mountain ash leaves its way into spring,
into the memory of roots, remembering
everything you cannot recall.

Spring is where you cupped your hands as a boy.
Flowing out of the sand cliff above the river.
Garter snake there in the grass. Glistening.
Translucent scales left after
the creature slipped out of itself
and into the water.

Light moves like this. Faster even than mind.
Your father buried beneath aspen and birch.
Your mother somewhere north of north.

Biography is what the river writes. Not about you. Not in Greek.
The snake still swims. Far bank still distant. Still there.
Crayfish in the shallows. All that's not gone
is you. No saint left so much behind

as the snake. Skin left. Like that.
Your fate will come, too. Everything
you fear and refuse
to fear.

Death has your eyes.

There in the mirror.
Nothing looking back at you.

Do you recall the voice that summoned?
That voice said wings. But it was a question.
Raven tail-feathers winnowing wind.
Measuring time by the dance of light
on this shoulder, and
that thigh.

Whose? You cannot say.

And there's the hum, the hum
of everything
the human mind forgot.

The blackbirds are doing it again.
Their individual spirits moving
as a single body.

Flight patterns are Chinese characters,
and Arabic script, and Cree syllabics.
They all spell the same word:

Winter.

Yes, the blackbirds are doing it again.
Somewhere beyond the horizon is what
they have dreamed for an entire season.

And while you, too, have been dreaming,
you cannot even name the things you have seen:
black horse, meteorites like a necklace of fire

across the midnight horizon. No stars.
And now, your spirit, too, is restless.
The shrinking light. *Not enough,* it says,

Not enough. I will starve
the way the old ones starved.

Even
the dogs grew thin, ribs
jutting, curved like a thin slice of moon,
lips peeled back to a grin.

And what can you say? What will your answer be?
What ceremony will you drag your heaviness into?
The lodge reveals the dark knowing of the body,

its practise of slow unbecoming, the becoming
of its own absence. Light extinguished like the light
of this fading day, slowly, almost imperceptibly

extinguished.

You heard a story once. A story about a man who shed his skin like a serpent. No, not like *that* serpent. The one in the garden never shed his skin. You suppose evil is like that. Without transformation. Always the same.

You do not understand evil, except you do. You do not understand serpents and the shedding of their skins, except you do. You do not understand your own desire to shed your skin, to strip the skins of others. Except you do.

You woke up this morning, and even though it's spring, the leaves from the Manitoba maples had been torn and drought-scattered by last night's wind. Those leaves were lying piled on each other, their bodies, their veins, pressed together.

Makes you think of a woman you once knew. She had a gift for words, made them dance like late-evening-light-on-the-ripples-of-a-river. You knew that river once. Still, today, it is called *Red Deer*, in northern Saskatchewan.

The woman worked in a comic book shop. She made words dance. She tried to kill herself with vodka and gin. Let me
begin again. You heard a story once.

Except that was a different story. A story about St. Francis. No, it was about Bodhidharma. They didn't know each other. Except they did. You understand boreal sparrows perching on your shoulders, eating from your hand. You understand lying down with a wolf, feeding it, to protect the villagers. You understand why Daoists accepted the teachings of the Buddha. Chan and then Zen. You understand, the death on the tree.

Except. Your people have died. The shaking tents and the teepees. The buffalo gone. The children. Gone. The guns. Sand Creek and Wounded Knee. Smallpox and whiskey, blazing their ways across the great plains.

Where are your mothers now? Your fathers? Why do you want to shed your skin—the brown and the white? Mixed like that. Mud. Brown waters of the pike.

Languages—the languages of all your ancestors—do they exist? Probably not. Except they do, like the rest of the dead and dying. They exist to remind us of all we have lost. kâhkiyaw niwahkômâkanak.

ON THE NIGHT OF MY FIRST BREATH

after Rodney DeCroo

Outside the Thompson General Hospital, the wind was thirty-one miles an hour. The temperature at twenty-seven degrees below zero. The pack of wolves had taken down a moose on the frozen lake.

My father was at the hospital at twenty minutes after 4 a.m. when I screamed for the first time, even though he had spent twelve hours at the nickel mine, had barely slept, and had to be back by 8. The smokestacks that night were spewing the lead and arsenic that were caked in my father's fingerprints the first time he held me.

I like to think of him in that brief time, holding his new son before he was, once again, breaking his back in the refinery, above ground but still in a kind of darkness.

After another shift, his wife and son still in the hospital, he ate a fried-dry pork chop and mashed potatoes with Libby's creamed corn poured overtop. He fell asleep on the couch while watching an NHL game. He doesn't remember the teams or the score. But he did dream.

In his right hand a Sportsman cigarette burned, tarring the air like the smokestacks. In his left hand, a nuthatch the size of his thumb. He knows the squiggle the bird's voice makes in the air is a child's scribble in the margin of a red-covered notebook in an afternoon math class. And he knows that voice is as thin as a winter willow. And he knows it is the sound of a farmer widowed too young playing a saw with a bow on the front porch of his clapboard house in northern Saskatchewan. Maybe it was a vision of his own long-gone father, or grandfather.

And he knows the voice is his own. The voice that will whisper in his ear, something he wants to but cannot quite hear, the day he lies down on the bed, alone again, for the final time.

7

Baring yourself to the northern Manitoba wind is as close as you can come to grasping the unknowable, as close as you can come to being a saint or a shaman. When I say *baring*, I also mean *bearing yourself. Into, and beyond.*

In that November, in your diaper and fur hat, you ran your three-year-old body away from your father after he had finished bruising the eyes and bloodying the lips of your mother, your brothers and sisters, while you cowered in a closet. While he raged through the house, slamming doors and punching walls, you fled out the back door past the sled dogs, chained and yelping.

At the edge of the alley, where it had stepped from the bush, a bear briefly looked up from the husky-cross it had torn from its chain, then ignored you and returned to its meal as you rounded the corner of the house and stumbled down Sandpiper Crescent, in Thompson, Manitoba.

You didn't know where you were going, didn't have time to think.

Today, in the darkness outside, the prairie wind is out of the north at 62 kilometres an hour. Shingles have blown from your roof. And this morning, you do not, anymore, expect to be a saint, to be a shaman. When the phone rings, as you fry a breakfast egg, the name-display reads *God*.

You grab the phone by its black root, black like the fur of that bear.

There is silence.

MUST ALL THE NEW ANSWERS
BE THE SAME AS THE OLD?

for James Oscar Lundy

Morning again. Still March. At least the merlins have returned—a
nesting pair, all wing-beat and screech, pursuing each other among the
spruce. There is ice on the creek out back. When you step onto it with
a coffee and cigarette, you know it will crack—the way bones do when
asked to carry too much.

You wonder if solitude is the correct geography in which to find what
you seek. If you have come here with expectations, you should know
there are no stories. Or there is nothing but stories, nothing beyond.
You will have to decide. Alone.

The dogs yawn and blink at the growing light in the east. Even with their
kindness, their tongues and noses, your mind is fragile as gossamer at
dawn. What do you remember from childhood? The heart of a northern
pike will beat for hours after it is cut from the body. Still beating, long
after you have picked out the bones, eaten the flesh.

You search for the beginnings of war and poverty in your heart, so many
years now—even before you were born, when your father blackened
the eyes of his mother. When his father drank whiskey all night in town,
with the grocery money, telling stories about the war. Your grandmother
sitting in the dark farm kitchen, while her eight children slept.

You wonder if death is symmetrical, that kind of beauty.

You know this is foolish, after men have seen bombed bodies—the
limbs of other men, their intestines, hanging in the roadside trees of
Sicily. Those were stories he never spoke at home. Something else you
remember—the fierceness in your grandfather's eyes, something akin to
fear, and the silence he bequeathed to his son.

You have never been in that kind of war. It is by splitting wood, birch for the morning fire, that you discover the hardness hidden in every heart. After breakfast, at your wooden table with a cup of tea, a book, perhaps some music—partitas for solo violin. As if a full belly, a few words, and Bach could bring you peace.

This afternoon, cloudless, blue sky, and nothing frail in the bright prairie wind, nor in the returning geese riding their hunger into the far fields.

Remember this: the world does not die and die without being reborn. But hearts can, sometimes do.

Thirty degrees below zero for two weeks without a break, and the dogs are going crazy, seeing the knots on trees as squirrels, barking and hoping beyond hope that the thing might make a run for it. Back inside the house, with near-frozen feet after only five minutes, they stare at the walls and bark at their own reflections in mirrors. And you, too, are bushed in your small home that's become a cell. Hermit's cell or jail cell, it's come to the same thing.

Whiskey-bored, bottles collecting on the countertops, multiplying inexplicably before your unfocusable eyes. You can't recall how there came to be seven forty-pounders, empty as your soul after days of this madness. Music's playing somewhere, a country drawl and acoustic guitar, maybe Townes Van Zandt, and you know you know the song, but nothing is clear to you anymore. It's the only thing that is.

Hallucinations this morning. Skin crawling with larvae, until you got a couple of shots into your bloodstream. That familiar burn in your throat and belly. Eighteen months of unemployment and twenty-some years of not being able to name your own history have led to this. No one's to blame, especially not your father who tried to save you. It's just the absence of conversation with your own dead, who are with you all the time.

And, sure, your mother left the reserve, left the bush, before you were born. Left her language to die on the trapline where there had been so much death. Pelts sold to the Hudson's Bay Company and shipped south to make mitts and coats. But though your insides, including your mind, are on fire, it's a fast-false burn. You have nothing that can keep out that cold.

It's at the core of your bones. Emptiness there like the hole at the center of the galaxy. The hole at the center of everything. It's what you don't know that might save you. It's the darkness of the lodge. It's the steady beat of the drum. It's the old man's face and voice, speaking low in nêhiyaw or Nakota. It's the heated stones and their stories from before human time began.

And if you locate your heart-mind, you will know, my friend, you will know.

Mid-September. Mid-morning. Three days before the north wind comes for the last, brittle, still-clinging leaves—a wrack and riot of blackbirds in the cottonwoods. You might imagine each bird's body, each wing, each feather is a stone-etched character, glyphs brought down from the mountain in thick-fingered hands. But you would be wrong. These black bodies as they take flight are musical notations from the underworld, each note a sharp. That kind of language. Orphic.

Soon the frost will come, and snow mounded like the ash of bones ground and burned. But, for now, the light is long and slow, slick, and viscous as your body after making love.

In the cherry tree, hunting insects, a single Tennessee warbler, the pale shades of a Morandi still life from another time and climate. Of course, today, nothing in the landscape is still, everything rushing toward a new season and a new kind of light.

Perhaps *this* will be *that season*—that time of life, in which what you have become, what you are, is what you will be. Is this the day you have been waiting for? Has memory—a horizon that recedes into the future—helped you get here? All afternoon, just outside the window, the world has been coming to an end, while you have sat with a cup of twig tea, reading a poem, or a letter from one of those who has left you behind in this world. They have stepped to the other side of a paper-thin sheet. You hear them rustling like mice in the walls.

Tonight, the first Harvest moon looms encephalitic just above the back fence. Combines churn late into the night, kicking up dust like buffalo. In an old pickup truck, someone, a young woman perhaps, runs jugs of coffee out to the fields. And the moon tugs at the dead in your blood, pulling them to the surface like bodies rising when the river-water slows around a bend.

These surfacings, too, are a kind of resurrection—ancestors in your blood refusing, finally, to be ignored. Their spirits bloated like toads, and loud, croaking their death-songs among the reeds of your sleeping mind. Fireflies and stars. Aurora and early-autumn cold descending.

Ice pellets clicking like a bird's clawed toes on the snow, hard-crusted from last week's melt, this week's freeze, and two white dogs asleep on a brown leather couch after being watered and fed, having gamboled about the backyard, barking at a neighbour dog and a squirrel perched at the top of the telephone pole just behind the back fence, apple trees and maples deep in thought, contemplation of *no-thought*, meditating on *no-mind*, and you, your being-in-the-world, circumscribed, once again, by memory, that old curse.

You are remembering Budapest, the long afternoon walk with that woman you love, across a bridge, from Pest into Buda, and now, together, you are lost—from The Rock Church and Gellért Hill, to a postage stamp park, a pond with ducks you cannot name, a young man beneath a tree taking a break from his skateboard with a sandwich and a joint, a young woman, tattooed and pierced, sitting on a bench, her mastiff unleashed and following his nose among low-growing willows.

After a sidewalk cappuccino at a rundown bar, uncomfortable wicker chairs, the sounds of afternoon drunks, arguing and gambling, drifting out the open door, you are back on the street, more lost now than before, a tall man who speaks no English but understands your situation pulls up google maps on his phone, tries to give you directions. You both smile and nod and you walk away no wiser. What you know is you need to find the river, follow the current, and it will lead you to the bridge you can cross back to the hotel, which you have come to think of as home.

You might wander for hours, days, or longer, trying to get back to where it was you began.

Home, now, is this small, stuccoed house, the shingles still holding on ten years later, broken tiles on the kitchen floor, the scent of coffee on the stove, of cigarette smoke on your fingers and clothes, of the large dogs who are your companions, and another scent you cannot quite place

—it is the scent of absence, all that's gone, all the things even memory cannot return.

You say, *Sickle moon*, although you have never seen a sickle, except once—a rusted, pitted blade—in the museum or was it the antique shop, in Herbert, Saskatchewan. The rutted, dusty, east-west strip of Main Street, an empty potato chip bag blowing by your feet as you stood alone having a cigarette, your lover having gone inside, and the July heat almost unbearable after the air-conditioned car. The owner, a forty-something man whose wife had left this *God-forsaken place* to live in some other unspecified small town with his eleven-year-old daughter he hadn't seen for a year. He had bad knees from a motorcycle accident and hobbled from behind the counter like someone twice his age. Retired from long-distance hauling for a company in Ontario to this store in the town he grew up in to be closer to home and his girl. He slept alone on a cot in a small back room with a hotplate to prepare the meals he cooked right in their cans.

You were on your way to Calgary to listen to folk music. Gillian Welch sang *The Way the Whole Thing Ends*. Justin Townes Earle sang *Harlem River Blues*. Sitting cross-legged in the grass with a few friends on an island in the Bow River, the water lately arrived from the mountains, surrounded by piercings, tattoos, and bandanas, the sounds of laughter, bottles clinking, and the sweet scent of BC weed.

A road trip with the woman you loved. You remember her name, but you won't speak it here.

Sickle moon an hour and a half before dawn on this December morning. You can see the dark face cupped in the thin line of reflected light, like a closed eye. The moon is in the southeast sky, just above the horizon, and Venus just there, behind or beside.

And while you would like to make these words precise, more accurate than mere thoughts or reimagined memories, you know it makes no sense to say, *The moon is in the southeast sky.* The moon is neither in the southeast, nor only in this planet's sky, and there is no horizon, just another illusion, and Venus is neither beside, nor behind, but so far beyond that you cannot even begin to comprehend what such a distance might mean. A beyond so deep that space is indistinguishable from time.

Last night, a great grey owl in the cottonwood across the street. This morning, seven rock doves clap their wings and glide through the mist-grey light of dawn.

The dead do not come in the form of birds, and if the birds come from another world, with their beaks and scaled legs and feet, they do not know it and neither do you.

Beneath the snow, the stones have grown tired of singing the old songs and take their seasonal rest, and beneath the ice-covered pond, salamanders consume their winter flesh.

A man should not dream of what is dead, or he might never wake; he might walk that path like a vein of silent, silver ore, winding its way among the dark roots of trees.

In your dream, you looked everywhere, but there was no finding her—she was not in your mouth, not in your clavicle, not in the hollow between shoulder and neck.

Dare you check in the airless rooms of memory, search the stagnant chambers of your heart? You know that you almost know, and you know that is as close as you will get.

Memory? A child splits kindling in the cold shed at dawn. A young man weaves grouse feathers in a young woman's hair. An old woman asks the wolf-willow leaves to witness her passing.

In the spring, you will bear in your hands your shorn, braided hair to bury in the prairie soil. This morning, seven rock doves glide through the mist-grey light of dawn.

And the wind forgets and forgets
without mercy.

for J.S.M.

The man is listening with his feet. Just before he falls to his knees. It is February, the month of slaughter—the wind and the cold.

Roots have forgotten the sky, and bears in their dens cannot even dream it into being. This is the season when all dreaming must cease.

There is no *I*. This is the lesson you must learn. The lesson you have forgotten and forgotten again since you were a boy. Since the time when leaves and rivers spoke a language you understood.

The flare of the white tail on the deer, just before you sight it and put a bullet in its heart, is one hand waving goodbye.

AN ANSWER TO YOUR QUESTION

for Charles Bukowski

6 a.m. Americans sitting in their cars, exhaust stinking the air.
Where are they going? They don't have a clue. Neither do you.
You just want them gone, skipping down the street,
like ten thousand years of dead leaves.

FILM POEM

You move the snow
shovel from the front
deck to the back.

The bullmastiff, Reta,
watches you, wondering
what you are doing.

It is April and there will be
no snow for some time.

You know these words
are marginalia,
not the stuff of poems.

So, you reimagine it
from the perspective
of a camera.

Let's pretend
there is a production crew.
Let's say
there is a director.

Let's call the director Bergman.
Let us imagine God is watching,
an audience of One.

And there you have it:
a poem.

    A man, a shovel,
      a dog watching the man and shovel,
      a camera's-eye view. And God.

You cannot have a poem
without God.

You have only
one moment of doubt
about the self, about the words
it attempts to weave into
something that might mean:

when the man puts the shovel down
on the treated spruce-wood back deck

the sound is that of a hand-drum,
and there is singing, the sound
of a coyote howl.

TWO REQUIREMENTS FOR REACHING THE GOAL:
TO BEGIN AND TO CONTINUE

for my father, Elmer A. Lundy

A small boy stands alone on the Precambrian shore of a northern
Manitoba lake, tears on his face, as his father pilots the aluminum fishing
boat away, toward the lake's deep center, the sun blazing on the surface
and glaring off the boat, like a vision of god in the boy's squinting eyes—
his father grows smaller and smaller in the distance, an inverse of the
way he will grow, after he dies, larger and larger in his only son's mind.

It's only a memory. It carries no meaning. Nothing that lasts. Just
another of those many moments in one's life when the world can look
with its own eyes at itself becoming. Do you see that each of us is at the
mercy of everything?

Many years later, standing in a field, the memory does not come back—
gone like a wandering dog on the trail of something invisible to you.
In the field, there is only the sky, the stars, only the night. There are
no windows, no doors—no peering through, no threshold—and you
are unsettled, unsure, at this very moment, of what is asked of you. No
audience here. No witness.

It is hard to know where your body stops and everything-that-is-not-you
begins. How to be human now—here, alone in the moonless dark? A
dark like that crow in the alleyway behind your apartment twenty years
ago, clutching another crow's head, just the eyeless head, in its beak.

When you try to speak these things, your tongue adheres to the element
it knows. Iron, and the bitter taste of rust and blood. In its thirst, your
tongue yearns for speech, or for a silence more compete.
There's something in your heart, you've carried it there all your life,

and, at times like this, you work hard to hold it like a bird in your open palm—you work hard not to close your hand into a fist.

Like each of us, you have seen too much. You've been hiding in a closet in your mind, hiding in the darkness of the tomb before the rock was rolled aside to find you gone. Like a fish on the ground, pulled from its watery home, your mind trembles, quivers, seized by the sway and drift of death.

Take your body home from the field—your mind will follow—wash yourself, smudge. Burn sweetgrass, light a candle. Now, think.

Grief is the constant tug of gravity in which everything exists, to which everything bends.

The prairie wind in the fields tonight—a miles-long tongue that holds nothing back. The scent of mountain in its breath.

Saskatchewan, February, full moon, forty degrees below zero, and fifty-kilometre-an-hour wind-gusts out of the northwest—standing outside at midnight, the twelve-foot cedar beside you snaps and cracks in the cold. You are alone. No woman sleeps in your bed, waiting for the comfort of your weight to settle in beside her. Those days are gone and almost, but not quite, forgotten. You have not become that holy yet. Perhaps that is why you seek out the frigid prairie air.

Your boots squeak in the snow as you shift from foot to foot. A train east of town roars, momentarily drowns out the sound of wind in the maple branches. The coyotes are silent.

The wind-driven air is pure and allows everything to pass through it.

The moonlight on the cold-crystallized snow reminds you of something you cannot name, something you have never been able to name. Perhaps you have been unwilling. Perhaps it is fear. Perhaps it is anger, or desire. You know you should seek the extinction of delusion, but instead you light yet another cigarette. You know you should seek the dharma as a medicine, that if you were wise you would go inside and smudge, cleanse yourself in the smoke of sweetgrass. You would give up your thirst.

Your heart knows and holds the key—meditate, live purely, do your work, be quiet. But this heart, in itself, is empty, as empty as the throats of the sparrows that have frozen and fallen tonight. In the glare of tomorrow's distant dawn, there will be only the testimony of silence.

And although your heart knows and holds the key, and although you are alone and not quite beyond loneliness, and because there is still a feverish burning in your mind, something in your bones keeps repeating, *There is nothing. There is nothing. There is nothing.*

Nothing to be added to what has been done.

ANOTHER POEM ABOUT THE WEATHER, WITH NO MENTION OF KEATS

And it's not pleasant: neither the weather, nor the poem. Minus sixteen degrees Celsius. Light snow coming down at a twenty-three-degree angle pelting your left cheek. North wind gusting to forty-one kilometres an hour making it feel eleven degrees colder than it is. Minus twenty-seven wind chill and steel-wool-grey light. And what's the point in knowing any of this? As with an unhappy family, each day of miserable-end-of-January-Saskatchewan-prairie weather seems to be miserable in its own way.

No one wants to read a poem about a pleasant day unmarred by a dark thought. You choose to stick with the weather as it is, not to dream of summer: sun and leaves, and flowers blossoming in the rock garden— the phallic thrust of yellow cone flowers and purple lupine into a sky that is, yes, a heavy-moist blue. The hum of bees carrying your mind, not into sleep, but into some state of barely-there conscious meandering, a kind of lazy-cat-eyed, wine-induced meditation. Those Asian monks, they knew.

A memory: the junior poets, two twenty-something women at the back of the room, mock the reading of the senior poet, a woman in her sixties: *You can't have a poem without moths or some bird,* and they cackle, their hands flitting at the ends of their hair as if to find a loose strand to weave into a nest. They are feeling unkind. And, now, so are you. One of them writes poems that are yet another feminist re-writing of the fairy tales. You know the story: *Cinderella in tall black leather boots, kicking some ass at the ball.* The other writes wry, sardonic poems about internet dating and pornography.

Today, in the cold, you are alone, except for the dogs and the ghosts, who keep coming around. Their breath is light. A cobweb in the coving at the top of the wall above the kitchen window shifts almost imperceptibly as if some spirit the size of a fruit fly has become caught. You sit with your tea and a piece of toast pretending to be some version of a monk, while the ghosts wander from room to room ever so slightly disturbing the dust on the stacks of books—the books of psalms and the spiritual how-to's—that will remain unread.

Later, if you look closely enough, in the dust you will see their already-fading fingerprints.

HERACLITUS, OR HERAKLEITOS: SPELL IT AS YOU WISH, I DON'T GIVE A DAMN

People dull their wits with gibberish,
and cannot use their ears and eyes.

A pot of coffee and six cigarettes into the day, and you're finally ready to see the world. 7:30 a.m., early October. It's Tuesday or Thursday, or some other day. At your age, memory is failing, in new ways and for new reasons, all the time.

Soon, you have to be at work, but aren't ready just yet. You are thinking about the book you were reading last night, up too late again, the three dogs scattered, sleeping on the floor, one or another of them occasionally lifting a head, blinking at you with a quizzical gaze, all the lights out except for the candle and your reading lamp on the dining room table. The book says that people can't look at the world, can't really see what's there, much less begin to speak, to say anything that corresponds to reality.

Epistemological and ontological problems is the way you put it to yourself, leftover vocabulary from too many nights, year after year, of sitting alone and reading, one habit you haven't been able to set aside the way you set aside the bottle with its own kind of flame, the whiskey burn in your throat like a summer-long-boreal-drought fire in a stiff, westerly wind.

The book says people can neither look, nor see. But a pot of coffee and a half-dozen cigarettes into this day of the week you cannot name, you see a female Richardson's merlin perched atop the power pole at the back of the yard. Her blue-grey hooded mate lights atop the fifty-foot spruce and calls. You think of Cohen's bird on a wire and wonder what it was he saw: blackbird or starling? You think it must have been a blackbird, that he was thinking of The Beatles and that poet, Stevens. You'd like to tell all the poets that the blackbird saw Stevens more than thirteen ways even before he sat down with pen and paper to make himself famous, again.

Cohen's gone now, so you'll never know, but the species of bird wasn't the point, you suppose. No, he was more interested in the ineffable, and although you hesitate to call it a soul, you think it must have been something like that. Still, you'd like to know what kind of bird it was, instead of it being merely a metaphor for a thing he could neither touch nor see, like a woman's body that is neither more, nor less, than a shadow of memory.

When the Greek from Ephesus says people cannot see, you know what he means.

But the way you cannot see is different from the way the neighbours do not see, too busy rushing off on their Wordsworthian getting and spending to take much notice of any winged thing that's not easily identifiable—as an angel from the bible, that is. A Michael or a Gabriel. And you want to tell the guy who wrote the introduction to the fragments, with his talk about archetypal modes of thought and a strikingly postmodern, deconstructive mind that, really, he's missed the point of why there's anything, rather than nothing at all. The rare and random descent into visibility.

You want to tell him, your neighbours, and anyone who'll listen, about accompanying a pair of parentless, nine-year-old boys to a sweat lodge ceremony—in the middle of the city, in the heart of the hood—the other day. How they sat with you—one on either side—through four rounds of darkness, and then light. And how, later, you sat with them on the garbage-littered creek bank and talked with a refugee from Laos, who was fishing for carp. Each passerby, out for an afternoon jog, glanced momentarily, apparently mystified, at two brown men and two brown boys in the tall, brittle grass by the barely-moving, mud-brown water. A detail none recounted to their family later that night.

All the light we can see is between four and seven hundred nanometers on the spectrum. Still, those two birds are worth looking at. In an hour's time, you'll be sitting with those boys again, as they pack their bags for school. When you tell them about the merlins, maybe the only story you'll ever tell them worth their remembering, something in their eyes will flare like the match struck to light the smudge, will spark like the dried medicines the old man tossed onto the glowing stones in the lodge.

Sitting together for a few minutes on the front step of a house, the three of you still carry the scent of that smoke in your hair. This afternoon's rain will wash it away.

Caught on the branch-tip of a Manitoba maple in the neighbour's backyard, a grey plastic shopping bag filled with wind looks like a dull throw cushion on the pale blue couch of sky.

What kind of spirit might lay its head down there for a nap? A creature with a bird's raven-black body and the square head of a Molosser dog—a mouthful of gleaming canine teeth in the place you might expect a beak to be. It grips its prey with the hands of a man. Is the creature something you have imagined or encountered in a dream?

You want to forget the things you may have seen with both your inner and outer eyes, since you cannot articulate which have frightened you more. You know inner and outer rub, one against the other. You can hear that scratching like the sound of a dragonfly's four wings vibrating together as it dies in the dry summer grass. Or like claws on wood, something in the night that wants to be let in at the door. Should you let it in? It might lap your cheek and, then, lick the pulse in your neck.

Solstice at 10:28 a.m. Sun directly over the southern tropic. You must believe in its return. Only a few wisps of cloud today, high and stretched thin in the upper wind. Some time ago you spoke with a woman about your desire to descend into a cave. Perhaps Eleusinian caves were what you had in mind. Or something more like Postojna, where the olm, the human fish, lives. Once again, the troglodytic desire to live in darkness, to be blind, to investigate that kind of sight.

Look, let me try to be direct. The world's in a hell of a mess—
temperatures on the rise, along with sea levels, and the air filled with
hydrocarbons. Two hundred species a day disappear, and the *Guardian*
article you are reading is from 2010. Quickly heat a cup of tea, light a fire
and the final beeswax candle. Try to be quiet and read. You know it will
make no difference, that the world doesn't need another poem, another
metaphor for St. John's *la noche oscura*. Still.

Outside the wind has picked up and snow has begun to fall. In the dark
frame of the frosted window, the glow of Christmas lights on every
house.

In the southwest corner of the yard, two blackbirds shriek and abandon the thirty-three-foot spruce, where the merlins have claimed last year's crow's nest. You watch until there is no *you*. Realize that, all along, self was a kind of nest, too. An emptiness, a hollow place constructed to hatch something else.

The stubby, brindle hound is warming up her howl as a train approaches. She knows the sound. It speaks to something in her gut and bones, while you think of Hank Jr. singing *If You Don't Like Hank Williams* because those are the kind of blues you grew up with. In that small northern town in the bush.

The summer air was thick with the sour-sweet scent of still-bleeding wood, when you and your father, in a yellow pickup truck, drove past the mill-yard piled high with logs. Where was it the two of you were going? You certainly couldn't have known you would end up here— treeless prairie—your fingers burrowing in earth, buried like your father, more than a quarter-century now. More than half your life ago.

You were coming from or going to your aunt and uncle's farm, north of town, just past the graveyard and the sloughs. Not a farm, really, just a small clearing where they kept a cow, two pigs, a scrabble of scrawny chickens, and a few thin horses. You and your older cousin, named after your father, ran through the low branches of willows with small-calibre guns at your sides. Abandoned cars and trucks from three different decades—scattered like carcasses in the dapple of sun and leaf-shadow.

Your cousin skinned the squirrels, stretched and dried their hides in a small, plywood shack that smelled of flesh and death. A dollar and fifty cents for each pelt. The rabbits you fed to the neighbour's dogs who always had pups. In their ramshackle house, there were as many kids as there were dogs in the yard. Spruce grouse breasts fried on the stove. Instant mashed potatoes and canned corn. The heat of that kitchen unbearable in August. And the stench—of sweating bodies and shit, cigarette smoke and cheap wine.

Just like then, right now, you have no idea where all of this is leading. A habit of mind—always trying to make sense of what never does. Why do you write it down? Try something else. Pick up a book. Read. *The Blue Cliff Record*. Dragon smoke in a dead tree. That's what memory is. That smoke. That dead tree.

Spring again. Trying to recall where you are. And who? And how? So many seasons of forgetting. Knowing, now, at last, the definition of poverty.

Wet, late spring last year, no cherries, no plums, the apples no larger
  than oversized peas,
still the waxwings and a single blue jay come, get drunk, shout at the
  sun.

After dark, a neighbour's head floats moon-like in the window above
  her kitchen sink,
hands moving like pale, lazy carp in the warm water, unaware you are
  seeing her.

The green ash, three feet thick, deep in Advent meditation, ten days
  before Christmas,
expecting nothing, no miracle beyond the hoarfrost crystallized on
  its branches.

Among the pile of fieldstones, lupine—purple, erect, circled by bees
  in late-August heat—
now gone to seed, more than you could collect in the brown-glazed,
  clay bowl on your altar.

After midnight, the dogs are first to notice the grey owl perched on
  the power pole,
a ghost in the corner of your eye, a wisp of cigarette smoke, dragged
  away by wind.

Today, forty degrees below zero in Pense, Saskatchewan. You watch the sparrows' frozen falling, one by one, from the branches of the spruce tree in your backyard, falling on the pitted and broken snow-head of the frozen earth. The rhythm of their falling is that one—the harmonica, the sway of a horse's hips, the sound of a lonely man's booted footfalls on desert sand.

For the first winter in your adult life, you have not hung a feeder for the birds. Perhaps you have forgotten your grandmother. Your Irish kohkum. What she taught you.

All that's been lost and forgotten—is there something else to remember, friend?

Back inside your small house, in the middle of a Beethoven piano sonata, the rev of a neighbour's Polaris snowmobile interrupts, but for a moment—or an eternity—the two rhythms blend. What does this mean?

When you were a young man, your father said to pull your socks up. It took you thirty years to realize that the metaphor was not a metaphor at all, just truth—it was a set of instructions. Just a few plain-spoken words, rather than Hebrew script on a papyrus scroll.

And you would like to believe that your dead are in heaven—north, south, east, or west, up or down. You would like to believe they are there. The problem with heaven is that it comes with no maps. And you've forgotten the seventh direction.

There is something black hovering above your head, coming wing-beat by wing-beat, toward your left ear. Neither bird nor bat, you have no name for the thing.

Today, the needled pine boughs creak in the cold, seventeen-below afternoon light. You do not hear quite what their voices are trying to speak.

To you, the sound is like a temple bell.

You have crossed the river in your mind. Having arrived, the wind offers only a numb uncoiling of cold, and you have not adapted. Still, you expected more than what has been given. How is it that you have come to this place? This barren place, where nothing has turned out as you thought it might, as you might have wished. You live in a haze, a fog that no wind can clear, having undergone another day, another day gone under. Nothing carried from there to here. Not even your name has come with you to this far side.

The slow, muddy-brown current, ice just beginning along the edges of the banks.

Your thought is silent like the snow falling into the bare branches of aspen and birch, sticking there and melting, falling drop by drip. Where you are you cannot even guess, and the gates to everywhere and nowhere multiply, mutely open and close. You cannot remember or imagine, past and future unreal and beyond reach, and the present is so deeply far away. Farther away, and smaller, than the human figure in a Chinese landscape painting. A stoop-backed journey leaving no trace of itself. Nothing ahead but mountains and mountains, and another river beyond the next.

And low cloud, broken, scattered like your mind tonight. Concentration
somewhere beyond you, maybe hidden where this afternoon's
pronghorn moved, the clump of aspen at the far edge of the field, when
they picked up your scent.

Your practise is to sip tea and try to look into the net of the world, the
web of things, willingly caught, eager with the desire to see what will
yank you into some element neither water nor air.

Your world is steeped tea, a cigarette, and four dogs. From thin cloud,
March rain tapping at the kitchen window, wanting to come in or calling
you out into the cold, away from your thoughts and the warmth of the
fire. Alone drinking mint tea after a simple meal—cold chicken, buttered
bread, and cheese. Outside the kitchen window, in the branches of the
spruce, a hunched sparrow half-asleep, drooping like a water-heavy leaf,
a seed still clutched in its beak.

It's like that, you think. But the clock on the wall ticks, and it's not like
that anymore.

Light a candle. Burn some dried plants. Beneath the floor, beneath your
feet, roots make tunnels with their thirst. This is the ceremony of the dark.

Life begins, and suddenly it is mid-life and you are walking on a barren
road, empty hands and pockets—nothing to guide you but the story of
where you have been. Where does the mind go when it seems there is
no way to find *the way*?

Remember hearing the owl in the darkness, lying in your tent on the
hard-packed earth of southern Alberta, near the petroglyphs, the
endless wind's writing-on-stone. The ancestors. A woman at your side.
Remember your grandmother filling the feeder with sunflower seed
for the waxwings. Remember your seventy-year-old mother looking

skyward, eyes filled with stars, giggling like a child. Remember the silences of your grandfather, your father. So many dead now. Remember and remember and remember, again.

Each of us will start new lives. Many times. The world makes one promise only—the beginning again will continue. Until it stops.

Earth and sky-as-wind will make a song in your bones, even in the bones of your fingers. The bones of each hand with which you planted flowers, gathered fruit, touched those you loved. It's the closest you will come to singing.

No omnipotent hand will descend to scoop and carry you. The jaws of a wandering coyote, your final resting place. This is your hope. We lose ourselves the way we lose the world—piece by piece, feather by feather, paw by paw. And sanctity. The way we lose that, too.

Thirty miles to the west ice rots on the surface of the lake. All winter the fish beneath the ice were not the lake's perfect, breathing thoughts. They were simply pike waiting for the thaw. The moon tugs a minor, land-locked tide in the lake. It does so whether or not you pray. Pray anyway.

What a wonder to be like a stone that lives in a stillness that is almost eternity. To be like the river—infinite configurations in the span of a finite life. You see so little and know so little, perhaps that is a kind of wisdom. But you don't think so.

Moonlight, warm breeze after midnight, tundra swans asleep in the flooded fields—even the prairie grasses bend down on their knees.

The moon is not
thin as a fingernail
clipped. Not quicksilver
quick, or embryonic slick.

Maybe pale as some woman's wrist,
veined blue, not like a bruise,
not that dark. Not dew,
at dawn, or a sliver of pearl.

Still, there it is, moored
in the black branches of
the white pine. Cool
and biding its time.

A month ago, a snowy owl in the middle of the grid road when you were driving home after dark, its eyes two perfect, full moons in the headlights as you slowed, before it lifted its too-thin, almost-spirit-now body into flight, disappeared into the February, snow-dark, stubbled fields.

Spring now, Cottonwood Creek in thaw, you watch a doe move slow as afternoon light. Her curved hooves leave quotation marks in the soft, clay-banked hillside—the language between those marks now vanished, now silent—her dun-coloured body concealed in the stand of aspen and birch behind the faded, broken barn in the distance.

You wonder if affliction is nearer to the truth of things. *No. Neither closer, nor farther than beauty is,* you think. Today, the memory of all your dead drove you to your knees. It is the best place from which to see the beetles in the dirt, each a black, hard-shelled casket that will bear your flesh into the next world, and the next. Study that. Practise that kind of knowing.

As a child, you tried to live inside the sound of river-water flowing over stone, but the world called you back. Now, the path has become narrow, very narrow. But not secular, not that, not quite. There are no deities to bring home, only a red field-stone, a white river-stone—but what more could you wish? Plant wolf willow. Plant buffalo berry.

The moon tonight cut in half. How did this happen? You suspect the winged maple seeds—perhaps their turning blades, after carving the blue afternoon, continued their fall through the body of the earth, out the other side, into that other world, sliced the moon like a ripened fruit. Orange.

You know this cannot be true. You know these are only words. You know metaphor does not change *what is*. Still your destitute eyes, your mendicant mind, gather it all in, grasp at some teaching from this seeing. Perhaps you are in search of a self.

The world answers back—in its own time, in its own way.

After midnight, unable to sleep, you stand on your front deck having a cigarette. Somewhere the sun crosses the equator. Down the dim-lit street comes the single-eyed, half-Manx, feral cat. He could teach you a thing or two about the nature of suffering. With his coming, the wind rises, sings the old songs, is torn in the branches of the elm, flayed like the fringes of a ghost-dance shirt.

Another late-winter afternoon chasing no-mind. Seek and you have already stumbled past. It's difficult. Try this. In the maple tree standing beside the back deck, where you sit with a cigarette and coffee, two robins and a downy woodpecker. A small hound raises her black nose, opens her throat, and sings when a train passes by. This is enough. If it is not, ask yourself why?

For one entire life you have tried to argue yourself out of a problem you have never been able to name.

What consumed your grandfather, consumed your father, and, now, wants to consume you, too. Is it anger, longing, emptiness? How will you find peace if your mind is filled with such things? Try this. In the cottonwood in the neighbour's yard, a single Brewer's blackbird, the first one you have seen since the fall, when something you could not sense gathered their sleek, black bodies into flocks that swirled like smoke and ash from the underworld. And then they flew there, just as they had once appeared. Gone for a season. That bird is trilling like the woman in the ceremony the other night when the old man sang and shook his rattle, the scent of sage thick in the heat of the lodge.

And what kind of answer is this? The comings and goings of birds? Smoke and an old man with his rattle and song? There you go, stumbling again. The birds are returning, just like all your dead. And each day the sun is a few degrees higher in the sky.

Not much. It will do.

SOMETIMES WE ARE ONLY A SPRING GARDEN
SOME DEITY HAS LEFT ITS BOOTS IN

for 'Little' Elmer Lundy

Early June, early morning. The apple blossom's white opening is not virginal, not that kind of birth, but that pure, the patches of deep red at its center not stigmata, but another kind of holiness. The bees hum, not hymns from another world. *This world*, they buzz, *it is. Just this.*

Red-winged blackbirds cling to the bulrushes at the edge of the deep pond beside the highway, on the long curve, just north of the graveyard where your father will one day be buried—it is the drive to your uncle's farm, you are eleven, your father, still young and indestructible, at the wheel of the metallic-forest-green, two-door '76 Chevy Impala, the windows down, his thick forearm resting in sun at the top of the door. As the car speeds by, the birds screech, take flight over water, flashes of blood streak the air.

In fifteen minutes, you will be tramping the edge of a field with your older cousin, peering into willows, aspen, birch in search of grouse—as happy as you will ever be as a child. For supper, lean, white breast meat, spiced, coated in crushed cracker crumbs, fried in butter.

Years later, in his small house in northern Alberta, your cousin lives alone, surrounded by death—the heads of deer, elk, lynx, black bear, with their glassy stares, mounted on the walls, in place of family photographs. Those long-past, warm October afternoons of shared solitude served as practise for adult life, for the men you would become.

The air is hot and then it's cold. Season after season passes like that— time passes not by us, but through. Each of our bodies, entire, yours and mine, like a window or a door. And each day the same as the one before—every day the world is a restless dog, always wanting, always coming in or going out.

Just think of the work our bodies do, while our minds are somewhere else goofing off. The body might wonder why spirit is always inside it, and everywhere at once. But it has other work to do. It holds its silence, and leaves jigsaw puzzles to the mind.

You will pass the day in your backyard, with the dogs, moving quietly among the blooming apple, the wolf willow, and the stones. You will drink coffee, smoke cigarettes and skip your supper, your fasting an act of attention.

After sunset, geese are on the move. In the dark of this moonless night, you want to follow them into the far fields and sleep. You want that kind of communion. Their voices the only sign they are here, passing through the late-middle-age of your life.

Of course, the mind is emptiness. A cleft. Take that as the first precept.

It's like this: beneath the belly and between the four hooves of the sorrel horse as it runs, pounding the earth like a drum, is that great emptiness, the nothingness of which Lao Tzu speaks, from which each universe arises. And, tanned by the root-twisted hands of an ancient nêhiyaw woman, the prairie is a hide tight-stretched in all the directions, even the ones you do not see. Silver sweetgrass braids hang at her shoulders. Should you set them alight?

That space beneath the horse is the nature and being of mind.

Tied into the hair of the horse's mane and tail are ribbons of every colour. This one is red. This one is blue. Each ribbon is a flame that flickers in the heat and the afternoon light. The kicked-up dust rises like the smoke of the horse's prayer. And if there is a language here for you to learn, it is in the muscled shoulders and haunches of the animal as it moves. Maybe this learning sounds easy, but it must come on its own. And slow. While you try to sing, always try to sing.

Your life is lived in the gut of an animal much larger than you.

Tonight, perhaps tonight, you might dream—the physic moon climbs into the branches of a cottonwood tree in a shallow valley by a creek; the leaves droop when the wind falls; and in the newborn silence, you hear the voice of an old man as he speaks words no one has spoken before. He tells the story of a mountain in the south and how your mind must go there and sit. For days, without food or water, it waits for the land to speak. The names are all there. Here. With you.

The names, they are all waiting for something, too.

The iris shoves its fist skyward, unfolds into a hand,
unconcerned, unaware even, of other blooms browning at the edges,
collapsing, finally, like a star, dying without any explosion of light.

A white dog lies in the shade of apple trees, grackles raising a racket,
and the dog asleep, breathing heavily in a dream—a dream of mountains
    and a fox
red in its mouth. In the dream, humans speak with the voices of angels
    and ravens.

A book lies open on a table on a backyard deck. A cup of coffee nearby, a
    cigarette
burning slow in a clear, cut-glass ashtray. A man staring into the distance
    of wind and sky.
The title of the book is a series of indecipherable glyphs. Each page a
    blank field.

And death comes like this: word after word, always the words crowding
    in to see
the disaster. The trees are no more than their rings, which cling as if to
    memory.
Death is a horse that runs constantly toward or away from what you
    think you know.
                        Another and another,

word after word. And the sky. And the wind.
And mind. A fist opening into a hand,
opening like an eye.

I.

The stars are bits of sourdough crumb. I am sorry to say they are not pinholes in dark velvet sky. They are the bits of bread that have not stuck in the beards of celestial beings. The stars are crumbs scattered across the dark and discarded plate of death.

II.

If death was larger. If the green elm in the middle of your backyard, as if you could own anything. If that tree could speak to you, it might say *My strong arms reach—even to your god.*

III.

The desert night is taking you down to a temperature with which you are not comfortable. Your body is not amphibian. The salamander of your spine. The toad your heart is. Not even they want to sleep with you.

IV.

You read a book once. It was Chuang-Tzu. It might have been an instruction. It might have been a practise.

V.

Your dead. Those are the only people you want to speak with and they keep coming around.

When you ask me
why I am angry, inconsolably angry,
I will ask you not to ask me such a question;
I will ask you to remember
sixty million buffalo
slaughtered in the nineteenth century
to starve the Plains nations,
to drive them onto reserves.

I will ask you to remember
the rotting corpses of bison,
the rotting corpses of
my missing and murdered sisters,
and aunties and kohkums and lovers,
and the rotting teeth of the children
fed fat on McDonald's.

I will ask you to remember the rotting stench
of every Indian man in every Indian bar
across the continent.

I will ask you why he's there,
why he's not someplace else
with his family.

I will ask you to remember
the dirt-poor rectangles of reserves
where the people were sent to farm
and the cold rectangles of the hood,
segregated streets, the city blocks
where our people are sent to die,
each shaped like a boxcar without cracks
between the slats to let through the light.

Rain for hours this January afternoon and northwest wind at fifty-three kilometres an hour. The temperature drops like a stone tossed into a black pond. The bottom's down there and, stubbornly, doesn't want to be told. Behind the low grey afternoon cloud there might be a sun. But no matter how many times the Stanley Brothers nasal-whine *Angel Band,* the only winged creatures around are three ravens hunkered down in the low pine boughs. The only spirit that's afoot is that wind with its beak that pierces everything, including your war-torn, amputated mind. And it has broken the seal. Everything you've hidden from all your life comes flooding in. A beaked spirit drags its talons on the snow-crust scroll leaving behind hieroglyphic hymns no one can remember how to sing.

A train whistle blows as the engine roars by just a block and a half south. And you are un-homed. The steel machine calls: *Come. Follow me. Follow me into the darkened fields.* And you want to go. Even though going means you cannot return, you want to go. You want to follow that retreating falcon cry into the night. And you want to bring with you everyone you love. But you will go alone. Because you want to know what Hank Williams knows the same way Cohen wanted to when he wrote *Tower of Song.* How low-down, how deep does lonely go? At the bottom of the bottle, you failed to find an answer. You discovered that inside you were as empty as a glass once all the Jack Daniel's is gone. All that was left of you was the shaking in your hands and the pain in your bones. A sense of how easily more becomes less.

And now, today, here it comes, again. Here comes that something that's always been consuming you—the way your yellow, whiskey-stink piss eats the white, white snow.

WHISKEY: A KIND OF ODE

a response to lines from Donald Hall

With apologies, I cannot agree with you, sage,
that whiskey is not so ruinous as rage.
They are bedfellows, twin birds in a cage,

and they copulate in unmentionable ways—
spawning the most debilitating of demons,
gargoyles, and sideshow freaks.

I've done my research, spending days
in the haze of whiskey's fire, its blaze
that makes of cocaine's torment child's play.

I have breathed with the breath of the beast,
looked deep into its gaze. It has come to know
me, and I know its name, most secret, holy.

There is no shame in being wrong, my friend.
There is shame only in falling from the bed, then
crawling back into that wretched stench again.

A SLIGHT WRINKLE ON THE POND

for Patrick Lane, teacher

A tremble, a quiver like the hide of a horse disturbed by flies,
near the flank or wither. Small breath of wind in pine-shadow, in
moss-dark, in fern-eclipse, beneath elms near the river, under the
high sand banks of an ancient, proglacial lake. From where this
movement of air? This world or another? The yellow pond lilies shift
imperceptibly. Almost. You take note, you, unperceived, perceive.
And if you feel the need, the desire for something under the pond's
skin, something unseen that controls all that you do see, look closer,
and there's nothing but the black eye of a leopard frog. It doesn't
recognize you for what you are. Stones lie sunk in the mucky bottom
of the pond, each consumed by its own weight.

There is a heaviness inside the landscape, inside the body, inside the
mind. A heaviness waiting heavily for nothing to happen. Nothing
does not happen. Always. Like a young person in the throes of a first
love, you are driven to experience what is impossible. And like he or
she, you, too, will be disappointed. Your heart cannot do what your
mind demands: give up belief.

Stand here at the edge and stare at the pond, the thick soles of your
boots sinking into earth. Soon the moon will arrive. You can call its
image on the water *a floating stone*. This changes nothing. Stand and
stare until you grow tired of the moon's look of astonishment, the
blank gaze of the dark water. You will find here no imminent birth of
a self as yet unborn.

Whatever book you hope to read was never written, and if it was, it
was not with you in mind.

You will stare at nothing until you learn it, or it learns you, as it will,
by heart.

Wind out of the southeast at seventy-three kilometres an hour blows birds' nests from the trees. Balls of sticks and twigs, bits of dog hair—like miniature tumbleweeds frozen to the crests of snowdrifts.

December in southern Saskatchewan. A different kind of desert.

Here, there is no deity to hear the spirit's pleas, unless you count the distant sun god at a forty-five-degree angle, falling daily further toward the southern horizon, its light barely visible through the low, fast-moving cloud. No succulents. Instead of cacti, there is only the thin reaching of wolf-willow stems, brittle at twenty-two below zero.

And what is it you are looking for today, if not despair—a sickness of the soul?

All you must do is look. There is nothing but the desolation of the season in every direction, as far as you can see—barren fields without any memory of the geese who flocked there to feed on scattered grain left on the ground after the harvest just three months ago. Ice pellets come in hard against your cheek like angels pissing on a parade no one would consider having on such a day.

And does saying that, the irreverence of it, move you closer to where you want to be?

If such a place exists, it is not here, standing at the edge of this small, prairie, cloister-minded town, each house a grey shelter against wind and deep thought. You think the place might be in some other world that you glimpse only briefly in moments of discontent. But your mind is always ill at ease. Your seeing is never more than splintered, fractional, a fragment of dream you cannot remember until, in a moment of weakness, a kind of sleep, it returns. But when it does, it is transparent—like steam rising from a cup of tea, a vapour that dissipates as soon as it appears.

Revelation, yes, that is the term for which you were looking.

Try this:

The place for which you are looking exists only on the six quill-sharp tips of the claws of the woodpecker, blown off course and bewildered, clinging with its toes to the bark of the ash tree.

And:

Try as you might, you cannot say what this means.

It is snowing again, as if the weight of years and the gravity of memory were not enough.

Four inches overnight and another inch and a half so far this morning. It piles up on your shoulders as you stand in the backyard; it piles up in the crooks of trees, on the black backs of hungry starlings hunched in the branches, and on the white dog—a one-hundred-sixty-pound Pyrenees—half-asleep near your feet. How long have you been standing here?

This afternoon, after days of cloud, the sun will come out, and the wind will finally drop. Still, you will refuse to be at ease.

You will think of your grandmother planting seed potatoes in the boreal-rich soil near the confluence of three rivers; of your eight-year-old mother on the trapline with her first dogs, three of them, pulling a child-sized sleigh; of your grandfather as a young man travelling up the northern prairie from Thief River Falls, Minnesota; and of your teen-aged father leaving the homestead for work in the bush.

You will think of mistahi-maskwa locked-up in Stony Plain bearing the pain of his people, and of Bodhidharma crossing the mountains bearing the teachings. The chief stared at the prison wall, and the monk stared at the monastery wall. Perhaps that is the choice we are offered: the wall at which each of us will stare.

Today, you sit in a hard chair and stare at the dining room wall, a cup of green tea steaming the window so that, even if you were to look, you could no longer see. Out there in that world is the empty field, row upon row of ice-crested waves, as if liquid water had flowed across the entire visible landscape and solidified. You know the impossibility of such a thing, but you think it anyway, your mind, once again, up to its old weesageechak tricks. In the distance, a stand of cottonwoods, aspens, and willows. Bedded down in the shelter, a few trembling deer.

These are the things that are real and, always, just out of sight.

On the power line outside your open bedroom window, mourning doves in early July practise the plainchant of mid-summer sunrise. 5:04 a.m. and you are half-asleep, the world beyond still half-dream, nothing more substantial than the shadow-shapes cast by a fire on the walls of a cave.

Are you dreaming of rock painted with horses, bison, and thin hunters armed with bows?

That waking is distant memory, now, and bears a precarious relationship to reality as you struggle to comprehend the dim end-of-November light. A bowl of soup, a piece of bread with cheese, and a cup of tea are your meagre defenses against an encroaching sense of futility.

Last night, driving west from Regina toward Pense, you saw a dead fox on the shoulder of the highway—red, its hindquarters pressed flat into the pattern of a tire track, and its pink tongue frozen to the twenty-degrees-below-zero asphalt.

It had become a useless thing, a subject not even worthy of thought.

You saw the sun drop from the gut of clouds low on the horizon—the oranges, reds, and magentas—a kind of birth moments before it tumbled into darkness. Of course, you know the sun never falls into darkness. You know this is a trick of perception, a trick of words. Once again, you feel betrayed.

The sun carries its own light, is its own star. A deity that worships only itself. A fusion of hydrogen into helium at its core. Is this the condition to which you aspire?

Here on the northern prairie, it is the land and you that plunge into night. No place here for desire, for eros. The land, in its white hermit's robe, has taken its seasonal vow of chastity; the fox's body is a vow of poverty. What is the vow that you will take?

You know what awaits the things of this world: a silence on every tongue.

You want to say, *The light at sunset* is *a dead fox's fur*, or *A dead fox's fur* is *the light at sunset*. You want to say something that makes sense to you. And while you think, one hundred trillion neutrinos pass through your body every second. What, for you, could ever be enough?

The things of this world are in deep retreat, and your vision, like the winter trees, has turned in upon itself. Everything in descent, like entering a lodge from which nothing will emerge—except the low-sound of prayer, high-pitched singing, and a seed-rattle in counterpoint to the beat of the drum.

Even the horn of the passing train is half-frozen this morning. A sound like a humpback whale calling, a mid-range phrasing. A song that is a cross between an ignored dog's moan and the slow draw of a bow across the strings of a viola. A low, open G Robert Johnson would recognize. Of course, that's not quite right, but, hell, it's thirty-one degrees below zero and the trees are snapping and cracking in the cold. Beneath the ponderosa pine the lawnmower you didn't put away for the season sits half-buried in the snow like a child's toy, abandoned, dropped from a hole in the sky, from another place and time.

You are trying to say what late December is like, what this morning is like on the northern edge of the great North American grasslands, at fifty and a half degrees latitude. When you rose from your bed, the sun hadn't even begun its climb. You opened the curtains and blinds even though there was no light. Still, something in the darkness recognized your face, called you by name. That's how you've been feeling these days, like those windows—like a black, blank eye. The lack of sight just another fact of life. The emptiness of your looking, a hollow thing, and without hope.

No fight left in you. If other seasons are possible, it's only the stones who remember.

Everything in the landscape has descended into stasis, and that's true of your spirit, your mind. All of life's ten thousand things move like the starling frozen on the ground beneath the now empty branches of the fruit trees. The bullmastiff feints a run at the bird, and when it doesn't move she turns and limps back to the house, pausing to lift one foot and then another. You draw a last pull off a cigarette and feel the knife-edge of air in your throat. Back inside, pour yourself a coffee to wash down a boiled egg, a crust of bread, and a leftover piece of pork. Sit alone. Think of nothing. See how easily it comes to you.

Beginning of March, an afternoon melt and then a north wind and a quick freeze at dusk. The particulate snow is crusted and sounds like crushed bones beneath your boots. The moon is full, opalescent through the low, thin clouds at midnight, and you almost believe that it makes something you might call spirit shine through your skin—a kind of terrestrial transfiguration.

Why are you awake and wandering in your backyard beneath apple trees? Since you ask the question, you assume there must be an intelligible answer, some *reason* reason can provide. You try to parse the landscape and your place in it but find your mind is parched, as if the late-winter prairie were desert and you gone there in search of something beyond your grasp.

If the occasion demands a metaphor, you might say, *My heart is a cactus slaking its thirst on the underground salt-water blood of the ancestors in my veins—my heart is a cactus ecstatic in its sudden, brief blooming.*

But those are just words, and you have worked hard at your unhappiness, for years have tried dying a little at a time, moment by moment like leaves in the fall.

Is there a flawed beauty in the other world? In this world, there is only flawed beauty, but, slowly, you are beginning to believe it is beauty enough, maybe more.

You could spend ten thousand lives trying to find the portal close at hand. Why concern yourself with the shades drifting in the underworld, when they are with you, all around you right now? Look, even in this dim light, the spruce trees cast shadows across the yard and the season's last northern lights hum and buzz as they sway.

A great horned owl, motionless, sits atop the power pole beside the giant cottonwood. It does not contemplate mortality. Not its own. Not yours.

The clouds this early evening are the ash-grey smoke of the fire that's
been burning in the long-gone-to-dust-now bones of your ancestors,
centuries in the ground—those who spoke nêhiyawêwin, and, yes, the
smoke from the fire in the bones of the buffalo, wolves, and grizzlies,
who also used to roam the northern prairie up to the edges of the
boreal, where plains become parkland, before the mixed deciduous and
coniferous bush sings with the voices of rivers and wind.

Today, you read in a book a poem by a woman you admire, a poem
about the inaudible movement of the earth through space. *No, that's
wrong*, you wanted to tell her. *What is beyond the range of our hearing
is not inaudible. Is not the same as silence*, you wanted to say. You think
she might agree with you. Or she might explain the statement as a
perspectival truth about the nature of what is human. Thus, its more
general untruth would emphasize the limitations of our existence.

It's not an answer you like, but what good would it do to tell the woman
the stories your mother tells you about growing up on that trapline in
the northern Manitoba bush, coming out just twice a year for supplies
and the temporary consolations of human company? No one would
mistake such stories for truth, least of all you. How long has it been
since anyone mistook stories for truth? When it comes to questions of
epistemology, what kind of threadbare answer is narrative?

Still, you think of your mother as a child, as she hides behind an
outcropping of rock while her father lights the fuse of the dynamite
to blast samples to take into the mining company's lab in the hope
of making a bit of hard cash to buy flour, bullets, and more dynamite.
Perhaps a store-bought rag doll for the girl. In the long, dark, solitary
hours of winter, while her father is away checking the traps and her
mother is chopping a hole in the lake-ice to draw water, the girl talks
to the doll.

And you, now, at your age and distance from that scene, cannot hear what the girl whispered to her doll. Did she call it sister, scold it for being disobedient, tell it the priest would come and take it to the far-away red-brick school? The girl told the doll stories. Now, you tell stories as well. And what good does any of it do? You sit alone, just as lonely as that girl, and you realize the only stories worth telling are the ones that help you create a self you can live with and die with, one you can embrace and call your own, though you know that's only a story, too.

The clouds this evening are the striated grey of the single owl feather you found in the dewed grass beneath the apple trees. The last light is fading in the west, and the way the clouds twist and separate, you swear there are wings beating just beyond them, wings that, like immense gravity, bend the aeons-old starlight. When you finish your final cigarette and rise from where you sit on the front step, your back aches as if from carrying a great weight

—memory that stretches beyond anything you can articulate, beyond anything you can claim.

END OF THE YEAR

for Ken Lundy

Just before dawn, coyote-song from the north field. Minus thirty-six
degrees overnight and sunrise at eight fifty-nine. Each day lengthening
by a single minute. Sixty seconds more light stolen from darkness.

By late morning, a lone Bohemian waxwing hangs inverted on the
branch-tip of the mountain ash. The Hanged Man. What you can divine
from the bird's presence is its mid-winter, end-of-year hunger.

Your heart, too, has its beak and claws. In that way, it, too, is spirit. It is
hungry, wants what it already contains. Its four, muscled rooms large
enough to hold everything that rises from, descends into the

void. And you know *contains* is the wrong term because sometimes the
heart overflows like a northern river when the weather warms. In your
memory, a thousand years ago, the breakup was thunderous,

like Odin awakening with a bolt from dream. paskwâwimostos
pounding its hooves on the stony path that leads down to where the
spring water emerges from the sand cliff and joins the river that moves

like time. It is in the bends and twists of the river's flow that it most
resembles time—the water eddies, turns and curves, curls back upon
itself. It twists like a strand of thread when an old Cree woman beads,

her brown hands knotted like the roots of a tree. Her fingers ache, yearn
for something you cannot name. You are alone today, except for the
presence of three dogs. It is cold outside. The birch wood fire

you build brings sweat to your brow. This is all you know: the song of
wild dogs and the cold, two eggs poaching on the stove, and something
in you as restless as the brindle hound whimpering as she sleeps.

for Christian T.

Snow for a third day in a row. *It's Beginning to Look a Lot Like Christmas* is playing on radios and droning from speakers, outside stores and inside shopping malls, around the world. A steady dribble of electronic buzz and babble, the only voice of god we recognize.

The flakes falling through the grey afternoon air are frozen spittle from the lips of stuttering angels reciting, in their makeshift heaven, another *hosanna* that will lead to nothing, their world deaf and silent, dumb and mute, a world as cobbled together as our own.

The sun will stand still on the horizon, even though we cannot see this until it is finished. All the words we use—axial tilt, rotation, precession—mean the same thing: the famine months are upon us. Longest night and shortest day, the unforgiving angle of the light.

The ponderosa pine gathers the falling weight in its branches, accepts what is given, what comes. There is a barely-whispered hush from the brittle needles, if you listen. Its six-inch-thick trunk is like the muscled body of a serpent beneath your bare-handed touch.

At midnight the clouds break for a few moments before closing up again. You see the moon like a cracked egg in the indigo sky, the yellow yolk surrounded by a pale, not-quite-white corona. At its center is an embryonic bear, curled, awaiting birth.

Dust motes drift in the sunlight that fills the window where there has been no light for three days. They are dander from the wings of the spirits that stay here through these cold, dark months. Some might call them angels, but they have the beaks of red crossbills, the feet of dogs. The skin of lizards beneath black fur and feathers. They don't recognize human faces, except out of the corners of their eyes, the way we cannot see some stars when we look directly, but only aslant.

They have their own names for each of us and each of the things we think we know.

Sometimes they reveal themselves in odd, unexpected moments. When the young delivery woman brings Vietnamese takeout to your door, her wrist slides from the sleeve of her jacket. It's an angry red, scaled with psoriasis, her nails yellow as cigarette filters. And it's not the woman herself, but you know something that has brought food to your door wants to reduce you to food, too. Its hunger is the same translucent blue that glows at the base of a flame.

What can you do when you have no words for things you know to be true? Once, in a beer and whiskey haze, you stood in an alley behind a motel in the Okanagan Valley. It had been days since you were sober. Still, you were not drunk. You knew the difference between the burn of alcohol in your brain and the hallucinations that come when the fire blazes out of control. Something came down the mountainside, then, and out of the tall juniper lining the curb. Some *thing* emerged.

You will not speak of it here. It looked at you and spoke in a language you understood. You will not repeat what it said. Not here. You haven't been the same person since, uninvited, it moved like a worm into your heart. It still lives there. In a crevice in the muscle that pumps your blood. Telling the story would do no good. There are some stories that simply must be lived. Lived with. Stories with teeth and claws, with mouths, and tongues like those of crows—who have come too close to what is human—split.

Just sit at your table. Feel the warmth of the light that might last only a few hours. Think of the summer long past. Think what the roots think when they are frozen, hard as stone. Somewhere in memory, at the roots' unbreathing core, they grip a stillborn child that in a season to come will rise from the cold.

End of July, two days of rain
after two months of drought.
The house is cold, the dogs lazy and bored.

You remember three brown eggs—
plucked for the pan by your father's paw-like hands—
in a white bowl sitting on the kitchen counter.
You have asked for everything and are ready
to accept nothing less.

Every man is broken open by a man,
a man who is still a frightened child.

None of us is just passing through the universe.
It passes through us, a car on a night highway
speeding through a small, lightless town
barely slowing down for a look.

When are the times we tell nothing but the truth?

You fall in love too easily—
with dogs, children, women.
A river, a stone, a hillside
of wolf willow.

Your spirit wears no masks;
your mind does not invent.

It is a dangerous thing to be
human. We are all in danger.
A danger to ourselves, each other,
earth and trees, sky and crow
and deer.

You walk as if you are not afraid. Each day your walk
is a lie. One foot before the other on the path.

You cannot even say what you believe,
if you could believe. Still you walk remembering
fist and fang and flight.

Don't you remember who killed whom?
It was you.

Anger loosens knots, ties its own
tighter noose.

Red-winged blackbird breaks its vigil on a cattail, takes flight,
red flash of wounded air. Turn your eyes to the river,
tune your ears to its pulse. Heartbeat
of water and stone.

One way or another,
the earth is after us.
Our mother will eat us.
This is no fairy tale.

What is that song on your tongue?
A war song or a love song?
It is seduction either way.

What are the crows talking about?
Death and hunger? What else?

Hatred seeps
from the pores in our skins.
Natural, like that.

Do we really believe
we have heard and spoken so many words
there is nothing left for us to learn?
Believe your eyes and ears.

You are thirteen years old.
The roof of the trailer is leaking
in a July thunderstorm.
Your three-hundred-pound father
sets out pots and pans
on the linoleum kitchen floor.

The years have fallen through you, body and mind
a residue of what once was, of once upon a time,
everything that's been left behind.

Is nothing concealed? What nothing?
That nothing at the very center of things,
especially at the core of these words.

Each and every sorrow is known.
Under the weight of rain, the grass lies down,
the thin blades bent beneath
their own hidden lives.

We have no light that is our own, no light
that isn't borrowed like the moon's.

In blood-gut something beyond hunger and reason.

Your heart, although it opens and closes, is not a window
    or a door.
It is a house. Four red chambers, earthen home.
    Earthen muscle.

If the stones in the rock garden seem dull,
it is only a lack of sheen, they keen
with minds slower, more exacting,
more luminous than yours.

Afternoon prairie—deer-hide scraped flesh-bare,
        stretched, and tanned by drought.
Walking a steep footpath on the hills, south side of
        Buffalo Pound Lake,
the abrupt hush of pheasant wings leaving willows,
fleeing your approach.

Grasshoppers gleam, the pale green of corroded copper.
An evening crow coughs, clears its throat,
cricket-song pulsing in the wrist
of the world.
Tight-stitch the windows and doors. The night wind
gets in, dust and moths, mementoes from beyond.
A rattle of dried leaves or seeds in your bones.

At dawn along the still-frozen edges of the pond
Canada geese and tundra swans awake.
The earth sprouts long necks, speaks
its own language. As they take flight
the sky opens and something
we cannot name
flies through.

The sun climbs down invisible steps,
walks on water.

Veined leaves and the arteries of trees carry news
        of the seasons
to an underworld of rock and root and bone.

On your drive down Seven Bridges Road
you stop to see the horses. The white horse
greets you across the barbed wire,
presenting its downy muzzle, a muscled flank
before disappearing into the evening shadows,
the darkening aspen and willow.
Its body like a foreign or a forgotten
language.

Sun-retreat into the dark of distant hills. Just like memory,
everything we touch and then lose.

In the morning
when you have gone, the white horse will return
from the open mouth of the underworld,
a mouthful of dewed grass in its gentle mouth,
the black dust of poppies on its shining hooves,
bearing sunlight on its back.

Do you remember the night at your friend's cabin?
Early autumn, the fire out at 3 a.m., the cold,
someone moving in darkness
to feed split birch
into the cast iron
belly of the stove?

The lake within a stone's throw
quietly muttering something
into whatever dream you were having.
The sound of the wind saying,
Water, wave, water.

In the dream,
a woman came to you
out of the shadows of apple trees
wearing moonlight like a white dress,
like a bride.

A high-speed geology of thought, tectonic shove
and shift of mind. Abrupt disruption.
Spirit talk.

You would like to believe
your heart never believed
the end of anything.

Maybe there is no way
to pass through this life, without
being lost over and again.

In spring, tongues of water
speak syllables that have shed their skin.
They have travelled the boneyards of our ancestors.
The trees with their rings have kept a record of everything.

The river says, *Yes*, and, *No*,
and it means both. Infinitely.

Autumn leaves down from the trees,
you sit in the empty palm of your house.
Spiders on their lace nets. Imperceptible breathing.
Eight eyes watching you.

Blackened leaves sink in the river's flow, no trace left
of the life of sun and bright blue air.

A flock of white tundra swans seems to pass
beneath stars, through the black branches of the elm.

In the light and shadow rippling on the side of the black-brindle
bullmastiff, you swear you can read the verses of the *Rig Veda*. The
opening *Hymn to Agni*. In summer, you walked with her to an
abandoned farm site. In the hollow beneath an uprooted cottonwood, a
racoon nursed her three young. Eight pupils dilated, took you in, looked
back at your looking. The mid-afternoon flight of a grey owl disturbed
from its perch pulled your eyes as surely as gravity. Your father was there
at your side. Your grandmother.

What is it the wind has written on the snow overnight? Etchings on what
was a blank buffalo-bone, porcelain-white field under a waxing moon.
Is it Mayan, Sumerian, pre-classical Sanskrit? It is another language
entirely. You wonder if it is your mind and not your eye that deceives
you. Your mind that flits like a nuthatch on the grey-brown bark of the
ash tree. You know that, too, is you; you are it. Tree and bird. Simple
formula. Whatever is inside is outside; whatever is outside is within.

For a moment, the bark on the tree moves, flows and eddies like water in
a river you knew in childhood. You are knotted by memory again. What
are the stones you carry in your belly that you cannot speak? We all have
bones composed of memories we did not choose. Even when you forget,
your dead remember you. Their eyes are everywhere and watching. The
dead speak and hear in infrasound, converse with thunderstorms, with
the shift and slide of tectonic plates.

Look at the tree. It, too, is burdened with memory: the eight-toed
grip of goldfinches leaving infinitesimal scribblings on branch tips,
indecipherable, like lichen on the sun-warmed sides of rocks on a hillside.
The tree remembers the birds' flight, wants to follow them to wherever
they have gone. Imagine it: black feathers growing in the place of spring-
pale leaves, and the lifting away, the surge of the thick trunk, long roots
dragging in the blue air like the still-dark hair of an old Cree woman.

Listen. She is singing.

The way the cactus stores water within its body, you store memory. It keeps you alive, while holding death close, as near as each breath. This one. And the next. That intimate. Walking in the bush as a young boy, along the river bank—the muddy Fir just where it empties into the Red Deer—letting the old water-and-stone song carry you into another world. Just a step past or into the aspen copse. The gaze of a whitetail doe naming you in a language you are still trying to learn.

Last night, just after midnight, a snowy owl in a silent glide beneath the lowest branch of the cottonwood. Like a ghost. Not like a cartoon figure, but like a real ghost. And you would know. You have seen them come and go through the back door of your home, left ajar for the dogs on warm summer nights. July. Sometimes they sit and watch you sip your tea, but they do not speak, unless it's an infrasonic rumble, something akin to the groan of a logging truck passing on a gravel road.

Yes, ghosts. Like the last exhalation of a miner buried in a collapse, the wisp-twist of breath, like a spirit traceable in the cold, deep air. A mile down in the dark ground. But you have never been in the bottom of that pit. How can this be more than imagination? How can it be a vestigial memory? This world, and the others, are like the rings of trees—tightly bound but permeable, composed of everything they are not. We, too, my friend, are like that.

There was a Swedish poet who spoke of a self breaking up in the evening, abandoning everything while the sun drops below the horizon. The light thin, fragile, the way a spider's web seems to be.

Daily you approach your own death, now, closer than you have ever been.

And slowly you have begun to see, to recognize you are the breaking up and the abandoning you have practised secretly—even a secret from yourself—every fraction of your life. You are practising it now.

Heavy-feathered, black raven in the left-from-fall harvest stubble
standing up through the barely-three-inches of snow at the field-edge
just off the grid road at the north edge of the city.

Beautiful day. Just minus seven degrees, no wind, and the disc in the sky
like a hammered-gold Aztec sunstone. A great Mexican poet might write
a whole book about that sun. The raven picks at a discarded McDonald's
bag, a limp french fry hanging from its thick glinting beak. At least
something that might be called *good*—a meal—comes of the fear, anger,
and greed that drives the kind of creatures we are—those who throw
garbage from the window of a speeding silver suv. And drives you and
me, too.

Can we be done with pretending? Fifty years old, now, two-thirds of the
way through your life, if you are lucky. Fifty years old, and your nêhiyaw
mother can't believe what's become of her smiling, twelve-pounds-at-
birth baby boy. What's happened to his self-confidence? What you know
is that everything you thought you knew, up until today, amounts to
nothing. You know nothing. Too well. You have found it at the center of
everything. Your own mind. *Emptiness.* An absence of anything called
spirit or soul.

You will get through another day without a story to tell.

At work, a young girl whose father died a week ago from a
methamphetamine overdose. You sat with her as she sat with an Elder,
who smudged the girl with sage and spoke in low tones of her own life.
Because the girl wouldn't speak. You and the old woman from a reserve
in the valley coaxed, but the girl said whatever sadness she had felt was
gone, had left her. And you imagined that departure like a bird fledging
feathers before its first flight. But what you imagined is not the point.

Sitting on the back deck tonight, a full moon visible through the end-of-February-bare branches of the cherry tree. *The poem might be better with cherry blossoms*, you think. But this is not that kind of poem.

That poem would have to be set in another season. Another time, landscape, and climate. And a white owl just dropped from the cottonwood in the neighbours' backyard. The three dogs bark. You know when it disappears it has flown into an adjacent world. But it is not a symbol. The owl is a real bird.

That's what you want to tell the girl.

Driving the grid road, the 730, from Pense to Regina, you hit a bird. Momentarily saddened for the useless loss of life, by the time you have arrived at work you have forgotten it, just as you have forgotten most of the significant moments in your life: your birth and death, your parents' names and faces, the feeling of being held in their arms. You have forgotten your marriage, the woman who was your wife, the names of all the children who were never born. You have forgotten the age of the male Pyrenees with whom you have lived for at least twelve years.

Later, in a parking lot in the city, a woman tells you there's a bird stuck in the grill of your Jeep. Snow bunting. Another small death, in a life filled with them. Each moment of every day.

You have forgotten the burn of whiskey in your throat, the blaze it lit in your boreal mind, and the sickness the disease brought—drought in your mouth, a barrenness of mind and heart. Spirit withered like a root. Hands trembling like brook trout in a clear stream.

Your whole life has become a history of forgetting.

Late winter, and you have forgotten even the dun-coloured stone that you dragged home from the river bank and what it told you. The stone has wings inside: neither fossil, nor metaphor. The stone has wings at its core. For aeons it has been dreaming its flight.

You have forgotten Bodhidharma's response to Emperor Wu, when he asked about ultimate truth: *Empty. Nothing holy.*

First, it was the plum tree. Then the cherry. The crab apples. Later, the mountain ash and the hawthorn. The maple. Each of the trees flowering in succession. And no one noticed. Least of all you.

A student once said, *Before I began studying, mountains were mountains and rivers were rivers. Once I had begun studying, mountains were no longer mountains and rivers no longer rivers.* The student also said, *After studying for some time, mountains, once again, were mountains, rivers, once again, were rivers.* You think, *Of course. Clever monk. That makes perfect sense.* And even if your friends were to ask, you wouldn't be interested in trying to explain—*It's like riding an ox in search of an ox,* Yuanwu says. This is not a form of arrogance, in one of its many disguises. You have come to recognize them. All those masks that tear you away from the world. The only thing you see is what's right now. The trees. Not, now, flowering. Leaf-flicker. Wind—stiff—out of the northwest.

4 a.m. this morning. You stood before the bathroom mirror. A stranger looked back at you. Then he left you standing there, while he put a pot of coffee on the stove to heat and stepped out onto the back deck of the house, into the just-then-beginning light, for a cigarette. It had rained overnight. Earth-sky mingled scent. Coital-creation smell. Later, the man picked up a small book of poems, and read: *The creek carries the sound of rain.* He thought, *Yes, that's true, too.* The woman's words arrive from the Ruby Range in the Yukon. Kluane.

Now, she is back in the mountains, nearly a mile above sea level. Another three thousand feet up the trees thin out and disappear. Dragon-trick. Nothing but jaggedness. A bit of lichen. A grizzly feeding on miller moths hidden in the darkness beneath rocks, where British Columbia becomes Alberta. Those misnomers that allow us to think we know. Or, are the mountains back inside her, once again? Right where they have always been. That's no metaphor. That's the *just the way it is* of Madhyamika. Even the *it* dissolves. Dragon-breath among the peaks.

She knows this. Years of writing the same poem, over and over, like a round-rolled stone in the shoreline palm of a glacial lake. The archetypal poem. Not the archetype in our minds but the one in our DNA. The perfect one that corresponds to *this* world, not the haze of some Platonic form. A poem like a sheep's horn tearing open the cloud's belly, low over the steep range. You want to tell her that mountains are mind. Trees are mind. Blossoms are mind. Mind is nothing but these things. Always a constant arising. She knows this.

The stumpy, brindle hound sings with the sound of a passing train. She sings Hank Williams singing *I'm So Lonesome I Could Cry* and Hank III moaning *5 Shots of Whiskey*. But, of course, those voices arose from the field-hollers of slaves and the songs of dogs. Like the three dogs you live with, who peer into the neighbour's yard, looking with their noses. They see a world just at the edge of your perception, one you suspect is there, one that trickles, once in a while, into yours. The dogs scent the human forms beyond the fence—where they reside, the fears and anxieties they carry in their hearts and think they can hide, the salt-thick waters of their blood, and the mineral-dense content of their bones. Even beyond the tall fence of time, these animals sense the whispers of ancestors whose names you don't even know.

You want to tell the woman these things. And that you placed a blue-glazed clay cup, half-filled with black coffee, on the altar this morning. For your father. He came quietly, shy like a deer—all three hundred-plus pounds of him—to sip the coffee with death-withered lips. He sat at the kitchen table, stared silently out the window, seeing his own reflection, or the field beyond, or some world he thought he could remember from someone's past. Someone he thought he knew. You lit a candle and burned sage gathered from the hillside along Cottonwood Creek, in the same place where you will bury the ashes of another dog you had to part with last spring. You stripped dried leaves from stalks. Stalks brittle like bird bones from the Dirt Hills, then wrapped and tied them with white-clay-coloured twine, the kind your Irish grandmother strung between stakes to make rows in her garden. Planting potatoes. Keeping order in a small plot cut into the boreal wild near the Red Deer River. Coyote memory, again.

You want to tell the woman that you have been reading *The Blue Cliff Record*. That what you read there makes sense to you: *Sunyata means the spirit of emptiness.*

You want to tell her about the seven pelicans, their black-tipped, white underwings ablaze in late-morning sun as they lifted off the slow, brown, silt-filled Qu'Appelle River, when you were driving out to Payepot Reserve two days ago. You want to tell her that the sunlight on the wings of those birds was like the glowing straight-up-into-the-sky rise of a beam of light an old man might speak about if he had one of those wide-awake dreams. That dream of an underwater lodge where the People were gathered, sitting, talking in low tones, so he couldn't hear what they were saying, though he recognized the language as Cree.

In the dream, the People sat in a circle on the valley floor beneath water, beneath the flight of a golden eagle riding the high air, the same way you sat with the other men and the boys—on a bed of vetch, wheatgrass, and sedge—on the walk to honour the slaughtered buffalo, pausing four times on the way to the big lodge where the dancing will take place for four days at summer solstice.

You want to tell her about Loon Creek, in the coulee along the highway, on the drive back home. How you could feel the emptiness that filled that space on your brief stop there. And how the emptiness was a presence, was *there*. Emptiness—inside, outside—filling everything to the brim, like the creek itself this spring when it overflowed its banks. She knows.

Right now, outside the back door, the wild roses bloom. The bees gather. This is the northern-prairie June's brief, pink-fleeting flirtation with eternity. And you find you agree with Blake: each of these bright particulars burst the mind-forged manacles—the now-shattered habits of mind.

Tells stories of northwest Texas and the bitter
clementine oranges she grew on a dwarf potted tree.
She tells stories of marmalade, chutney, and vinaigrette
made from the juices of each small fruit, a colour
somewhere between sunrise and autumn.

She speaks of the sacred preparation of food,
the sacredness of taking it into your body, how
the earth walks around on your feet once you have eaten.
She speaks of how well-, carefully-prepared food
is the same as well-crafted sentences, the right image,
a metaphor that might properly speak
our experience of the world.

She tells you these things. And you know she is right.

Everything is there in her words. Everything is here. You can
        put your hand there.
You can smell the orange tree blossoming in spring after a
        winter indoors.
You can taste the coming rain in the air, on your tongue. Imagination.
Everything is here.

She dreams of oranges, an abandoned garden, and of cacti
        in the high desert.
In the dream she knows she shouldn't touch those spines.
        And knows she must.
You remember doing the same thing in your grandmother's
        house. Each time you
visited, you would press fingertips on her potted plants for the
        simple pleasure
of watching your own welling blood. What delight the
        forbidden can bring.

In that far away time, the woman did not dream the dreary,
    grey spring of the north.
She did not dream late April on the northern prairie. Saskatchewan.
Six inches of snow and the dark-eyed juncos searching for seed
fallen from the feeder. The sun's return slow, but steady.

Today, the ponderosa pine you planted a decade ago has begun
drawing water from the underworld, bringing sap toward the sky,
budding, and once again preparing for the nesting robins.
Some of the young, as they fledge, will fall into the mouth of a dog.
Some will survive. You will be heart-broken, awestruck.

In part, you are wrong; in part, you are right
is the advice she offers for living one's life.

And the words of that Elder keep returning to you:
You don't know what you don't know.
And you don't know what that means.

A men's fancy-dance drum is pounding in your heart-mind.
Chopin's piano is leaping and slowing in your ear. And you know
everything is here. The dead. The dead are here. Right now.
They are in last year's leaves still clinging to the Manitoba maples,
stirred by the slightest breeze this afternoon. The dead walk
among us, always. Even as you read these words. Listen—

you can hear their silences between syllables. In that moment
that is not a moment, between inhalation and exhalation.

When you smudge your body and mind, the smoke rises
beyond the sky that we call *sky*. It forms Cree syllabics,
Chinese characters, and Arabic script.

You can read all of these and none. You don't know
what you don't know.

And the woman dreams of oranges. She dreams northern prairie.
She dreams of a place that is there and here. She dreams,
and you dream with her of a place beyond the suffering
that causes this wheel to spin.

WOMAN, WITH A BROOM

With a yellow, straw-bristled broom, red and blue thread woven around the top, the woman, nun-like, sweeps the debris of dried leaves from the cement pad at the back of the house. The kind of broom no longer commonly in use, which she must have purchased at a Peavey Mart, where only the older generation of farmers shop. Before her an ancient Hungarian woman lived in the house. Now, the woman lives here, alone, with her shepherd-cross dog. And the ghosts. Of the house. And her own.

It is spring or autumn—it is hard to tell—and, as always, there is work to be done in the shoulder-season, always something to prepare for, some coming or going, even if she cannot see what it might be from where she stands, swaying at the hips in rhythm with the swish of the bristles, or moving her feet in a slow shuffle, a kind of meditative, solitary waltz. Perhaps the woman's hair is the colour of sunlight, gold-spun web from the abdomen of a between-this-and-that-world spider, and just as fine.

Beneath her breath, she hums a song that only she knows. It's a loose version of a jazz standard—Thelonious Monk—but is completely her own. And, at the edge of sight, she spies the dark-eyed juncos whose bright, white outer tail feathers bring her delight when the birds scatter. She feels blessed by the presence, at the feeder, of white-capped sparrows and common redpolls, which are merely passing through the northern prairie, on their way to or from boreal nesting sites.

It is the brevity of their presence in her life that brings her joy, a kind of letting go that is a freedom she would like to embrace. But this is a thing more easily done with birds and seasons than with lovers, parents, nieces and nephews. Of course, she knows, we don't get to choose. *Perhaps that's how a life is composed, like a poem,* she thinks, *in the acceptance of the things we do not choose.* And she concentrates on the motion of the broom, and the slight, quick motions of the birds.

And she knows it is her own human weight that causes the bristles to bend to her will and do their work, her work. The work we have all been given. Still, as evening approaches, on its gleaming hooves, with its softly greying muzzle, she feels as if she might float away like smoke from an extinguished match or from a grassland fire, or the way the waning moon floats away in the close, growing-ever-closer sky—

Late October, a few degrees below freezing, full harvest moon rising
orange from fresh-cut fields east of town, geese settled into the evening
stubble, stomachs filled with fallen seed, a pack of coyotes stalking in the
dust of furrowed earth, Tennessee brindle hound, nose to the ground,
leading you directly toward that hand-drum climbing above the horizon,
northwest wind eagle-whistling on the power lines parallel to the east-
west run of the rail tracks glinting in the light.

You are tempted to call your walking *ceremony.*

Ancestral memory in your feet and thighs: in blood, bone, and marrow.
Your heart is a muscle-lodge, animal-alive with its murmured prayers.
Your visible breath is smoke from wood-stemmed, stone-bowled pipes,
four of them, passed from hand to hand, from lip to lip. The wrinkled
hands and withered mouths of those who have gone before you along
this path. All this inside you: what your body knows before your mind.

Back home in a small house with a bowl of soup and a cup of tea to wash
it down, three dogs asleep at your feet, you are alone except for their
breathing and your own. Whose face is that lit, skeletal reflection in each
window where you stoop to consider the gathering dark like the folding
of a crow's wings? Take a seat and all your dead come to sit with you,
hungry ghosts; their moans rise from the fire as split birch empties itself
of moisture—snaps, cracks, and curls, slowly becoming ash. Set aside
the *Suttanipata.* Toss tobacco into the flames.

Think of the monk who takes off his shoes in the temple's doorway,
enters, and returns to put back on his shoes. He repeats this, again and
again, each minute from dusk until dawn: take the shoes off; put the
shoes on.

The mountain ash has retained every one of its leaves deep into
this winter. You cannot understand it. You think there must be an
explanation, but there's that nagging question again: *Why?* Why must
there be an answer, except what is? In the wind tonight, the leaves rustle,
a sound like rubbing the dried wings of a dead moth between your
forefinger and thumb. They crumble to dust, and you press an ash-grey
print on your forehead to let the world know where you have been.

It is not a sound from this world except during times of visitation, a
sound like the brushing together of frost-glazed angel's wings when they
perch, just outside the kitchen window above the sink, in the brittle-
thin December branches of the fast-asleep willows. Once again, they
are disguised as pine siskins in search of seeds. You know the birds are
simply birds, but also that the glint of the weak sun on their beaks and
claws is a light angling in from a place you cannot see.

This afternoon, you sat in a coffee shop in the city. You were reading a
book; it was the *Chandogya Upanishad*. All the worlds were meeting in
conference on the street corner outside, but you looked up a moment
too late, saw only a homeless man with a shopping cart stuffed with
plastic bags, one filled with clothes and a woolen blanket, two others
with cans and bottles. Around his feet circled a single pigeon, staggering
like a wounded veteran from the war in the heart of each of us.

Twenty degrees below zero but no wind. The snow layered the man's
few belongings and the green canvas hat pulled on over the red
toque on his head, white flakes drifting into his black beard like the
crystallized thoughts of extinct deities. And you knew the man was you,
that you stood outside and wore his face, while he sat comfortably in a
leather-bound chair sipping a seven-dollar coffee. That is not true. All
you could do, what you did, was hand him three cigarettes and a few
coins as you left.

Return from memory. You are standing in the yard. Turn, now, go back into the light of your home, out of the darkness of this night. Light a candle and try not to fight the sense that you are that and that is you: the deer bedded down in the aspen stand across the field west of town; the rising, just-days-past-apogee moon; and Aldebaran, the bull's fiery eye. The ten thousand things remain; difference is not erased. Neither is the guilt, nor the pleasure of being the kind of creature you are.

Stare into the flame at the tip of the braided cotton wick. In this moment, you feel the breath of everything. Everything, this near.

Mid-November. After record-breaking cold, a warm front arrived overnight from the southwest.

Even though the moon had pulled on its black monk's robe, you were standing in the yard just after midnight when the wind dropped like heavy, velvet drapery at the end of a performance, and everything held its breath as if in the presence of some spirit that demanded it.

Cleared sky, star-shine, and the slow fade of northern lights. The air as still as the inside of a fourteenth-century cathedral in Catalonia—Santa Maria del Mar—except not stale with paper, prayer, and death, not an atmosphere composed of the breath of priests with dust and ashes on their tongues.

The night air was warm, but crystalline, clear, and dense as jets from the nostrils of a horse after a run.

This morning stalactitic icicles hang from the eaves—shed skins of angels left behind as they moved from one kind of being into another, vestigial. You think perhaps the angels have become waxwings, now congregated in the fruit trees.

Out on the deck with coffee, you notice a tiny spider, three or four millimetres in length, suspended at eye level by a single filament attached to a low-hanging spruce bough. The creature sways back and forth in an imperceptible-to-you current of air. The spider is trying to get somewhere

like a person—let's pretend the person is you—in a boat on a river,
adrift after he drops the oars and spinning until he can no longer
distinguish the far bank from the near. He falls asleep and into a dream
as deep as a spell: the man stands alone in the prairie night, and as the
sky revolves,

you are dizzyingly in love with it all.

Yipping from a coyote hidden somewhere in the stubbled field at the edge of which you stand. Three canine yelps that remind you of Peter three times denying Christ—*thrice* as the scriptures put it. But, of course, you've got it wrong, once again.

Canis latrans denies nothing. Prairie wolf. It raises its voice to praise the ascent of the last-quarter moon as it climbs into the cloudless, star-filled, end-of-November sky—turning it ink-blue. As it rises, the moon continues its monthly slide into darkness.

The air is only three degrees below zero, but a stiff wind out of the south-west is cold on your bare face. Are you here looking for a way to repent, or is it merely that wind bringing tears into your eyes?

You are middle-aged now and wondering what hope the coming years might hold. Your left knee aches from the walk on the ice-covered village streets and then the narrow, rutted road that brought you to this place. With each passing day, more of your life becomes memory—what is near seems to erode, to fade and lose its shape, while the past looms larger and becomes more defined. All that you have done, and have failed to do, is a growing weight on every thought and mood. The past holds you close as if it is the only horizon toward which you move.

In the far distance, you hear the groan of a diesel engine. Andromeda is tangled in the branches of the maples near the tracks.

The coyote yips again and is answered by another nearby. Soon they are joined by two, and then three more. They begin coyoteing, a kind of yodeling that becomes a powwow song—a deep-throated singing, climbing quickly to falsetto, to which you must listen until you know their howling is a yes that is only a yes.

Let it be so.

For just a moment, in the chilled air, you find it is not your body but your mind that becomes like a comfortable coat: you wear it easily, and slowly you unbutton and loosen it, until it scarcely weighs on you at all.

Mid-September and wasps are finding their way out of the cold and into the house. You hear their hum matched to the hum of fluorescent lights, above cracked white tiles, in the kitchen where the kettle, set on the stove for green tea, is about to scream. You catch each insect in a clear glass, cover the open end with a piece of blank paper and free them at the back door. You read: *How deeper than elsewhere the dusk is in your own yard.* No, that's not true, you think. Not even true as a metaphor for your own entry into middle age, one giant step closer to death, the night that *drifts up like a little boat.*

This evening, a thin drizzle causes ash leaves to droop. Some drop. And you find yourself wanting the *Ding an sich*, the thing-in-itself, not simply the memory of things, which is what the cold and snow will bring. The dog you euthanized this spring, now ashes in a cardboard box on the mantel above the fireplace, and your father dead now more than a quarter-century, buried in boreal soil. You want the woman sitting cross-legged at the end of the too-low-in-the-water dock at the end of summer, practising Ashtanga, asanas and pranayama, near the edge of the Manitoba escarpment, while the lake water laps and evening light leans, comes down the slope, with its muzzle, to drink. You want the brush of the wing-tips of the warbler on your shoulder as it darts around the corner of the house, rushes by you like a breath.

You want an angel to descend and come to understand that this is where it should have been, always: among the fermenting apples on the ground, surrounded by flies. You want an angel with granitic feet and its head filled with a swarm of blackbirds, flocking, each cell in each dark body pulsing with one word, *migration*, an untranslatable Morse code tapped out by the sound of a single brittle leaf tumbling in wind down a gravel-grey street. You want to be in the Cypress Hills, touched shyly, at the base of your neck, by the lips and nose of a horse, a horse that will not approach your looking but comes close when you turn your back and stare into the distance of aspen and pine.

You want to be blessed, like a man standing *just off the highway to Rochester, Minnesota*, who is held in *the eyes of those two Indian ponies*, and who if he stepped out of his body *would break into blossom*. You want the simple truths of *small red potatoes boiled in their jackets* for dinner, and *the salt shaker, the glass of water, the absence of light gathering in the shadows of picture frames*. You want to resurrect vegetables fresh from the garden in your own body. Transubstantiated. Transfigured. You want to know the dirt that peers from your eyes. Darkness into darkness.

Even though you know *it does not require many words to speak the truth*, you want a list of some things you lack. You want to sit beside the fire, in a soft chair set just within the circle of light and warmth cast by those flames. You want to name, but be still, and still be, grateful.

Years ago, in a poem, you spoke of *claws clicking across shingles*. They were the curled, sun-cured cedar shingles of a retreat house where you were trying to sleep after giving a reading to a group of mostly ranchers and other artisans. Men and women with work-calloused hands. They nodded and politely clapped, went away with the suspicion you wouldn't know how to help birth a breeched calf.

What is it you think you know? What were you trying to tell them, dear one?

You thought the sound that night was the light of the moving stars. A kind of music of the spheres. Maybe it was just dried leaves blown from the branches of maple and cottonwood trees down in the valley, at Eastend, Saskatchewan. Maybe it was angels dragging their scaled tails as old, at least, as the T-Rex bones meditating in the white clay cliffs washed in moonlight.

There you go again, adrift between metaphor and common sense.

Let's try it another way. With your eyes closed to the world, another world opens. Like an old barn door, repurposed, that slides noisily on a track between rooms in an otherwise silent house. Maybe you mistake that door for nothing but a wall, but it isn't like that. Not like that, at all. Even when you are not looking, light seeps in through the cracks—at the top, at the edges and beneath.

This morning, you are older and still know little. Still feel the ache in spirit and bones.

Here you sit, in your own small house, drinking coffee and thinking of the men and women in that auditorium. Reverend John Wilkins sings *Jesus will fix it.* And you know that whatever god might be, it has come to you on four padded feet, shoved its black nose in your face, wants to put its pink tongue in your bowl of split pea soup. What more could you want?

In the dog's eyes is a simple desire. Something you might learn.

What would you call the sky today—cerulean? Well, it's blue anyway.
Quite a gift this early, Saskatchewan March, after weeks of cold and
wind and low grey cloud. And what about the clouds today? Would
you call them pearl? Well, they are not, but they sure are white. And
the temperature is above zero for the first time in months, and there are
waxwings in the backyard picking among the remnants of winter apples,
shrivelled and almost black. The brindle hound-dog is singing with the
passing train, a song that to you sounds plaintive, but she is happy and
hopping in the softening snow, and your own spirit would like to howl
along with her.

If you could forget what's not real. If you could let go of your own
clinging and grasping. If you could recognize your self for the thirsting,
aggregate thing it is. If you could learn a few things from the birds
and the dog. If your mind didn't tremble and quiver and flit wherever
it desires and wasn't resistant to restraint. If you would gather good
teachings, as a skilled gardener gathers flowers, or a careful cook
gathers herbs. If being alone is better than being led or leading another
astray. If your mind didn't make itself the enemy of your heart. If your
heart did not make itself an enemy of the day and the moment. If
letting go allowed for an unbinding. If you are a lodge built of bone
and blood and skin.

KINTSUGI

for Nathan Mader

Slate-grey, late-autumn sky, end of October, and rain, light drizzle but as thick in the air as the aphids were just a week ago when the weather was still warm. And you know you have written that phrase before.

You are repeating yourself. All the stories you tell are the same, not even slight variations these days. This is how much your life, your seeing has narrowed, contracting like molecules of moisture as the temperature drops. Only a handful of words, like the tiny, black, dried seeds you gathered from the lupine today.

Now, you sit in the chill of the house, the fire unlit, staring out the window, watching a wolf spider trapped between the inner glass and the outer screen. And you tell them over again like counting and recounting beads on a mala—

your teen-aged father, not-yet-quite-a-man, blackening the eye of his mother with his fist, down at the barn, while his father was away in town to buy some nails, or sitting in the hotel bar drinking foam-topped glasses of beer with his buddies from the war until the resurrected memories blurred. Or your mother away binging for three days in the bars of that northern mining town before returning to your father with his fists clenched, heavy as ball-peen hammers that he put to work putting her in the hospital. Or your brother stealing your money and car after a night of drinking in The Barry on 20th Street in downtown Saskatoon, how you tracked him down at a house party the next day and didn't hit him, even though you wanted to. Hank's *I'm So Lonesome I Could Cry* barely audible through static on the radio and the swaying bodies of strangers everywhere when you took your first, deep pull from the neck of the Jack Daniel's bottle.

Slate-grey, late-autumn sky, you say, burdensome as memory, as the weight of flesh—skin, blood, and bones. And your mind, again today, spinning like a wheel in the mud. And what, exactly, have you said? That the sky is heavy, grey and cold as stone? Do you expect anyone to take that as an adequate metaphor for your spirit, your soul—fine-grained, foliated, homogeneous metamorphic rock. Clay and volcanic ash. Everything that you are.

Listen, my friend, yesterday I sat on the back deck with a cup of coffee and a cigarette, the three dogs jumping and barking at the circling of a half-dozen broad-winged hawks, just above the tops of the spruce trees, all of them the rare dark morph. And, it's true, I felt something close to joy. Maybe it was simply a kind of peace. I don't know, and I am comfortable in that unknowing.

I remember just something in me lifting like a wing, rising like the voices of the dogs as they leapt and danced on their hind legs. Something in me was pieced back together like a fine but shattered Chinese porcelain bowl. Not healed, just not quite broken in the same way anymore.

LINES WITH NO OPINION REGARDING
INDIGENOUS MYTHICAL REALISM

How to explain that the two jets of hot air blasting in your face come from the nostrils of a buffalo standing before you in the darkness of the lodge? The wings of a large raptor beat in and brush against your left ear. And fireflies flicker in and out of existence—subatomic particles—before your wide-open eyes. Why would anyone believe these things if you cannot yourself believe?

Some things should not be talked about. Not talked about in poems. Isn't that what you have been told?

Still, you speak here only to the dead, or the nearly so. The buffalo are gone, long ago, back to the dust and ash of the prairie. Feeding the grass that once fed them. And you, too, my friend, are gone across that great river. Stone by stone the water walks into the distance. This world is not your world anymore. As you read these words you, too, reader, are fading like the light at dusk across the open broad fields.

In *The Blue Cliff Record*, you read: *In one there are many kinds; / in two there is no duality*. Of course, you think. You've always known this is true. You want to write letters to Plato, Boethius, and Augustine regarding the medieval problem of universals. Invite them to sit with the old man from Carry the Kettle, who runs the sweat. He could tell them a thing or two. Nonsense, non-sense, you say, dear reader.

How is it that you and I have met here on this page? How is it we have met this day?

Did you know I came here specifically to meet and tell you that a peregrine in its black executioner's hood sat on the power pole just beyond the back fence this morning while I smoked a cigarette and sipped some coffee. The air was thick with mist at 6:35 a.m. when a slight breeze swept aside the veil and there perched the bird. Remember, I speak here only to the dead, or the nearly so.

Time to put these words down. Return, now, quietly to our other lives.

Epigraph from *The Brihadaranyaka Upanishad,* taken from *The Upanishads,* translated by Eknath Easwaran, founder of the Blue Mountain Center of Meditation, © 1987, 2007; reprinted by permission of Nilgiri Press, P.O. Box 256, Tomales, CA 94971, www.bmcm.org. The Sanskrit title can be translated as *The Forest of Great Wisdom Upanishad. Upanishad* can be translated literally as *a sitting down near or beside,* the way a student might sit near a teacher, and refers to the collection of ancient texts comprising part of the Vedas.

Epigraph by Charles Wright from "Looking Around," in *Bye-and-Bye: Selected Late Poems.* © 2011 by Charles Wright. Reprinted by permission of Farrar, Straus and Giroux.

Italicized line (with an added line break) on page 19 is from Patrick Lane's "Ars Poetica" in *Washita,* Harbour Publishing, 2014.

Heraclitus quotation on page 29 is from Brooks Haxton's translation, Penguin Classics, 2003.

Arbeit macht frei on page 51 means *work sets you free.* The German phrase appeared at the entrances to some Nazi concentration camps, including Auschwitz.

The Swedish poet referred to on page 78 is Pär Lagerkvist; the book is *Evening Land.*

The Mexican poet referred to on page 79 is Octavio Paz; the book is *Sunstone.*

On page 82, the quotation "The creek carries the sound of rain" is from Elena Johnson, *Field Notes for the Alpine Tundra,* Gaspereau Press, 2015. The title of Johnson's book inspired the title for this book.

The two italicized lines in the first paragraph on page 98 are excerpted from "After Reading Tu Fu, I Go Outside to the Dwarf Orchard" from *Chickamauga* by Charles Wright. © 1995 by Charles Wright. Reprinted by permission of Farrar, Straus and Giroux.

The first three italicized lines in the fourth paragraph on page 99 are from James Wright's "A Blessing" from *Above the River: The Complete Poems and Selected Prose*, © 1990 by Anne Wright, published by Wesleyan University Press and reprinted with permission; and the last two in the same paragraph are from "The Simple Truth" in *The Simple Truth: Poems by Phillip Levine*, © 1994 by Phillip Levine, used by permission of Alfred A. Knopf, an imprint of the Knopf Doubleday Publishing Group, a division of Penguin Random House LLC, all rights reserved.

The italicized phrase in the final paragraph on page 99 is attributed to Hinmaton-Yalaktit ('Chief Joseph'), a leader of the Nez Perce.

The italicized line on page 100 is from Randy Lundy's "Memory," *The Gift of the Hawk*, Coteau Books, 2004.

The italicized line on page 105 is from Randy Lundy's "Memory as a Record of Loss," *Blackbird Song*, University of Regina Press, 2018. Kintsugi, also known as Kintsukuroi, is the Japanese art of repairing broken pottery with lacquer and, also, a philosophy that affirms brokenness and evidence of repair as an integral part of the history of an object.

The italicized line on page 103 from *The Blue Cliff Record* is Thomas Cleary's translation, Numata Center for Buddhist Translation and Research, 1998.

Randy Lundy is a member of the Barren Lands (Cree) First Nation. Born in northern Manitoba, he has lived most of his life in Saskatchewan. He has published three previous books, *Under the Night Sun*, *The Gift of the Hawk,* and *Blackbird Song*. His work has been widely anthologized.

ᐅᓄᑲ

OSKANA POETRY & POETICS
BOOK SERIES

Publishing new and established authors, Oskana Poetry
& Poetics offers both contemporary poetry at its best
and probing discussions of poetry's cultural role.

Jan Zwicky—*Series Editor*
Randy Lundy—*Acquisitions Editor*

Advisory Board

Roo Borson   Tim Lilburn
Robert Bringhurst   Daniel David Moses
Laurie D. Graham   Duane Niatum
Louise Bernice Halfe   Gary Snyder

For more information about publishing in the series, please see:
www.uofrpress.ca/poetry

Amelia
Dellos   MFA Columbia
College
Chicago

9 780889 776913